TIPPING THE

sustainable management of world resources

dr john wright

BECKETT BK KARLSON

First published 1998
by Beckett Karlson Ltd
The Studio
Denton
Peterborough
Cambs PE7 3SD

A catalogue record of this book is available from the British Library

ISBN 1 901292 02 9

Produced by

Beckett Karlson Ltd
by Beckett Karlson Ltd
The Studio
Denton
Peterborough
Cambs PE7 3SD

Design & Layout by Paul Holness
Illustrations by Marc Lowen and Dean Hill
Printed in England by Page Bros, Norwich

This book is dedicated to my father
John Haig Wright 1918 - 1996
who gave me my great love for books and reading

FOREWORD

The original idea behind this book was to fill a gap that existed between more learned books and papers on the environment and the often depressing reports that appeared in newspapers and other similar publications. It seemed some three years ago that, particularly in the public domain, too much emphasis was being placed on doom and disaster and not enough on the positive changes that are taking place in how people view and interact with their environment. Many people wanted to know what they could do to help to protect the environment. Many were concerned that we seem to live in a "throw away society". The pollution of our environment by our waste products and the using up of the Earth's resources were the causes of some considerable worry. This book therefore tries to provide its readers with an introduction to a number of environmental issues associated with pollution and the production of waste. Emphasis is placed on the importance of waste management which is both environmentally and economically sustainable. The relatively new concept of sustainable development, a "more for less" approach to resource management, integrated waste management and life cycle analysis are all presented, it is hoped, in an interesting, informative and appealing manner.

The intent was never to frighten readers with tales of how badly mankind has done in the past but to show how we have learned from our previous mistakes. The main intentions are to underline the importance of maintaining and improving our environment, to increase an understanding of why we need to treat it with respect, and to suggest ways in which people can make their own contribution to sustaining our environment. If waste can be controlled in an economically successful way then less will be taken out of the environment and the potential for pollution via emissions to air, land and water greatly reduced.

Many of the examples quoted herein are not original and are better reported in the books and papers listed in the Further Reading sections at the end of each chapter. The author hopes that he will have initiated and encouraged his reader's interests in environmental matters, and made them think a little more positively about the future of their world.

Those boxes labelled Fact File provide extra information on some of the subjects mentioned in the main text. Words appearing in italics are explained in the Fact File boxes or are to be found in the glossary.

The author would like to extend his thanks to Mr. Alan Henderson, an Environmental Officer of Ryedale District Council, North Yorkshire, who often acted as a sounding board for some of the material. Thanks must also go to Mary, Matthew and Beth Wright who spent their valuable time reading and supplying constructive comments as each chapter was produced.

A very special thank you is extended to Professor Christopher Butler of the University College of Ripon & York St. John who gave his full support and considerable help to the author throughout the writing of this book. Without his careful proof-reading, encouragement and interest it is very probable that this book would never have been completed.

Finally, where opinions are expressed within the pages of this book they are those of the author.

PUBLISHERS' ACKNOWLEDGEMENTS

The publishers would like to thank those who helped with the content of the book:

Figure 1.1 - 51 Clarke Avenue, Derby: Reproduced by kind permission of the County Archivist, Derbyshire Record Office. DRO D 4773

Figure 1.2 - Aral Sea: Reproduced by kind permission of NASA.

Figures 4.1b and 4.1c - Harewood Whin Landfill Site: Reproduced by kind permission of Yorwaste.

Figure 4.2 - Thermal Treatment - The Teeside Energy From Waste Plant: Reproduced by kind permission of Cleveland Waste Management Ltd.

Figure 4.3 - Biological Treatment - Scarborough B.C. Organic Green Compost Process: Reproduced by kind permission of Scarborough Borough Council.

Figure 4.2 - Thermal Treatment - The Teeside Energy From Waste Plant: Reproduced by kind permission of Cleveland Waste Management Ltd.

Dr Peter White, Principal Scientist, Global Technical Policy Department, Proctor & Gamble Technical Centres Ltd.

CONTENTS

INTRODUCTION

the physical state of our world - is it really as depressing as we are led to believe?

Global warming, it is claimed, is being caused primarily by man's actions that have resulted in the pollution of our atmosphere by so-called greenhouse gases. If things do not change then our polar ice caps will melt and the sea will rise to a height such that only the tallest New York skyscrapers will stick above the surface (so states one American school textbook). Other pollutants put into our atmosphere are causing acid rain which is destroying our trees and forests. Organic farming is much better than using pesticides which pollute our rivers, killing living organisms and causing cancer in humans. Billions will starve because the world's population is growing so fast that not enough food can be produced to feed everyone.

Lack of resources! Increasing pollution! Overpopulation! Scenarios like those described above may lead some of us to believe that perhaps the end of the world is nigh, or at the least living conditions even for the so-called first world countries are seriously at risk. We are, to use a rather hackneyed expression, "all going downhill fast"! Where is the truth in all this? Is it possible to determine what is really going on?

This book certainly contains many examples of where things have gone wrong in the management of our environment, by both industrial and commercial concerns as well as by members of the general public. Many other publications have illustrated how mankind has depleted the world's resources and how badly its air, water and land have been polluted by human actions. Since the early 1970's, many newspaper headlines have claimed that the world is facing various environmental catastrophes. On the other hand, since the early and mid-1990's some books have been published which seriously question the truth of such headlines. The authors of these books have been called "contrarians". Reviews of their work have tended to focus on the fact that they question some of the positions taken on environmental concerns by environmental organisations and, indeed, governments.

Reading newspapers, watching television and listening to the radio could easily lead someone to conclude that there are only two positions to take in the environmental debate - either we are well on the way to an almost inevitable world catastrophe or there is nothing to worry about at all. This book rejects both of these viewpoints.

In truth, the contrarian view is not that there is nothing to worry about, but rather that many of the concerns that people have are not proven problems. Perhaps too much time, effort and money have been spent on possible problems, and this has led us to be too relaxed about the real, major problems, such as the disease that is spread in developing countries because drinking water is not properly disinfected.

Equally, many environmentalists such as Greenpeace recognise the importance of focusing effort on the real proven problems. However, they need to capture the imagination of people so they will become members of environmental organisations and provide the money that they need to pay their staff and fund research and publicity. One problem here is the biased and emotional views that can emanate from these organisations (as opposed to the biased and economically led views of industrialists!).

How are ordinary people to know the real truth? It must be admitted that this is not easy. For example, scientists honestly disagree on the interpretation of the available data on such important issues as whether or not we are experiencing global warming and climate change. All scientists agree that the amount of carbon dioxide and other greenhouse gases in the atmosphere are increasing. It is perfectly possible to measure their concentration. All scientists agree that these gases absorb and re-emit infra-red radiation which has been emitted and reflected by the earth. This so-called greenhouse effect has been around for millions of years; it is why the earth is at the temperature it is. Without it life as we know it couldn't exist.

Beyond these agreements the difficulties start. There is not enough data available to measure whether or not global warming is actually occurring. Certainly, the warm temperatures of recent summers in the UK, for example, are not outside the range of historical summer temperatures. We can say, though, that there have been more warm summers since 1980 than we might have expected. Our problem is that temperature data has only been kept for about 300 years - not very long when you consider that life first appeared on earth about 3.6 billion years ago. Attempts have been made to estimate what temperatures were over a few thousand years ago by measuring ice rings from plugs of ice drilled out of the Arctic and Antarctic. Unfortunately, although these show the occurrence of various ice ages and warm periods they are not precise enough to help us to unravel whether or not the past few years are within past experience. Still less do they help us understand cause and effect relationships.

In science, determining cause and effect is very important. We can observe and measure effects. When we understand what causes the effects we can predict what other effects may be caused and we can do something about them. If we do not properly understand causes we might do the wrong thing out of ignorance. This is why scientists are usually particularly cautious.

To help to provide further understanding on global warming, some scientists are trying to model our climate mathematically. They use powerful computers to calculate the effect of various factors, including greenhouse gas concentrations, on temperatures and other key climate factors such as annual rainfall. The work falls into two parts: building a model that can reproduce what has happened and been measured in the past; then using the model to predict what will happen in the future. Great progress has been made with building such computer models, but even with the best of them the agreement with past events is not good enough to be sure they can predict the future.

The debates between scientists on these issues are every bit as intense as a debate in the House of Commons, although generally perhaps the scientists are more gentlemanly and focus more on the facts! If even the scientists cannot agree amongst themselves how our environment has been changed by man's actions, what chance does the ordinary person have of understanding what is going on? Most people can only try to follow these debates and attempt to form their own opinions by reading articles in informed magazines like New Scientist or Nature and by reading some of the books that have been written. There are few, if any, easy answers.

Yet events do occur where the environment is clearly damaged or people's health suffers because of environmental problems. It is from such events that scientists try to learn so that things can be handled better in the future. Very often it is events of this headline-grabbing type that lead to new laws. Voters demand that something be done to ensure that the problem never occurs again. In such circumstances, politicians need to be seen to be doing something or they may not be re-elected at the next election.

Sadly, actions taken and laws passed in the immediate aftermath of a headline problem are sometimes not the best that could be done. There is a tendency to act without all of the facts being available or all of the ramifications being thought through. Recently in the UK the sale of T-bone steaks was banned because of worries over BSE and related diseases. Some would consider this to be an ill-informed law passed "after the horse has bolted". Some would say it is an infringement of their civil liberties!

This book takes a very pragmatic view in looking at one area of environmental concern - resource usage and waste prevention and handling, whether it is waste going to air, water or land. By reducing waste less material and energy resources will be used and the amount of pollutants entering our environment should correspondingly decrease. We look at some of the genuine environmental problems that have occurred - many of which were briefly in the headlines - and seek to draw lessons from them that can ensure that fewer problems occur in the future.

In taking this approach I am taking a middle course between extreme environmentalism and the contrarian view. I believe that I am taking a view that is held by a significant number of people.

It is a harsh fact of life that people learn from mistakes. There is a simple, logical reason for this. If nothing happens, it is impossible to know whether that is because all appropriate precautions were taken or because nothing would have happened anyway. When something happens we can seek for a cause and try to ensure that the events leading up to that cause are interrupted in future. This is the essence of environmental management - based on what we know, we try to organise matters so that if we predict something harmful will happen then we can take preventative action. Everyone, at all levels of life and in everything they do, can apply this principle - everyone can be an environmental manager!

Incidentally, most scientists believe that if the world does get warmer then the sea level will rise between six and forty inches. The USA now has more standing trees than it did in 1920, and more trees are planted each year than are cut down. World wide, trees are also being planted to replace those that have been harvested or destroyed. Fruit and vegetables that we eat contain more natural *carcinogens* than are added by pesticides. The world's population is growing but food production has increased at a faster rate and looks set to continue. It is war and misguided government policies that are the most important factors leading to starvation.

Now read on!

Further Reading

At the end of each chapter you will find a list of magazines, journals and books which will expand upon what you have read. There are three scientific magazines which are easily accessed, *New Scientist*, *Nature* and *Science* which often carry articles concerning environmental policy issues and scientific reports. In addition, there are a number of other journals such as *Ambio*, *Environment*, *The Ecologist* and the *National Geographic* which are also well worth looking at. *Chemistry in Britain*, obtainable from a Royal Society of Chemistry member, contains a news review section and the occasional article on the environment. If you are particularly interested in the control of waste, then *Warmer Bulletin* published by The World Resource Foundation will be of particular interest and value. You will not require a deep understanding of the more complex concepts of science to understand their content. You may find some of the recommended books quite difficult in places but still manageable.

N.Alexandratos, *World Agriculture. Towards 2010*, Food & Agriculture Organisation of the United Nations, Chichester, England, John Wiley & Sons, 1995

B.N.Ames & L.Swirsky, *Environmental Pollution & Cancer; Some Misconceptions*, Rational Readings on Environmental Concerns, Ed. By J.H.Lehr, New York, Van Norsted Reinhold, 1992

B.N.Ames & L.S. Gold, *Pesticides, Risk & Applesauce*, Science, May 1989

D.Avery, *Global Food Progress* 1991, Indianapolis, Hudson Institute, 1991

L.Bernstein et al, *Concepts & Challenges in Earth Science (3rd Ed.)*, Englewood Cliffs, NJ, Globe Book Co., 1991

R.Doll & R.Peto, *The Causes of Cancer*, Oxford, Oxford University Press, 1986

K.D.Frederick & A Sedjo (Eds.), *America's Renewable Resources: Historical Trends & Current Challenges*, Washington DC, Resources for the Future, 1991

J.J.Houghton et al (Eds.), *Climate Change 1995: The Science of Climate Change*, Contribution of Working Group 1 to the Second Assessment Report of the Inter-government Panel on Climate Change, New York, Cambridge University Press, 1996

E.Lawrence et al, *Longman Dictionary of Environmental Science*, Harlow, Longman, 1998

M.Sanera & J.S.Shaw, *Facts Not Fear*, Washington DC, Regenery Publishing, 1996

CHAPTER 1

TWO CAUTIONARY TALES
a big bang and a dying sea

Several examples of the mismanagement of resources, and waste treatment and disposal are presented to provide reasons for the need to conserve resources and protect the environment. The chapter emphasises that the needs of society must be counterbalanced by less waste production whilst appreciating that waste will be inevitable. An effective management style based upon an environmentally and economically sustainable approach is suggested.

In the early hours of the morning of 24 March 1986, when most of the residents of Clarke Avenue, a quiet cul-de-sac in the small town of Loscoe in south-east Derbyshire, were fast asleep, a huge explosion suddenly rocked the neighbourhood. The occupants of Number 51, a husband and wife and their son, were trapped under the rubble of their totally destroyed bungalow. Fortunately, all were soon rescued and taken to hospital, where it was found that the wife had suffered a broken arm and a fractured pelvis, while the husband and son escaped with only minor injuries.

Thousands of miles away, in the Central Asian Republic of Kazakhstan, the sleep of many inhabitants was disturbed by the effects of cancer of the *oesophagus*, *hepatitis* and diseases of the *gall bladder*, stomach and *pancreas*.

What was the link between these two clearly disastrous situations? The answer, as we shall see, may well lie in the management (or mismanagement) of natural and man-made resources. Let us now look at the two situations in more detail....

A BIG BANG: OR HOW NOT TO MANAGE SOLID WASTE!

Figure 1.1 51 Clarke Avenue

Initially, the cause of the explosion at 51 Clarke Avenue was thought to be due to a methane gas leak (cf. Fact File 1.1.) from either a faulty gas appliance or the mains supply. Thus Gas Board Officials were amongst the first people to arrive on the scene. Later that morning representatives of the Local District Council,

Derbyshire County Council and British Gas also visited the site. Tests carried out in the surrounding buildings by British Gas officials showed the presence of high concentrations of methane gas in two other bungalows (44 and 59 Clarke Avenue). These were immediately evacuated. Samples of the gas were sent for laboratory analysis and the contaminated buildings ventilated by knocking out the air-bricks below the floorboards and opening the windows. Tests carried out that day showed the composition of the gas which caused the explosion was different from that of the domestic methane gas supply (cf. Table 1.1). The latter was thus not to blame, so where had the gas come from?

Close to where the explosion occurred there was a landfill site that had been used for a number of years for the dumping of waste materials. It was known that such sites could be a source of gas emissions containing methane and so further investigation of this site was suggested.

By 26 March 1986, the mains gas supply had been conclusively ruled out as the source of the explosion. Scientific evidence supported the suggestion that it was caused by the movement of methane gas from the landfill site. The explosion was believed to have been the result of a sudden, unusually large fall in atmospheric pressure that allowed a large surge of gas from the landfill site to travel along cracks and fissures in the sub-surface rock strata and through drains, eventually accumulating under the suspended floorboards of 51 Clarke Avenue. When the central heating boiler came on at about 6.00 am, it also ignited the methane and air mixture contaminating the property.

Continued examination of properties in the vicinity of the explosion site showed only a few were polluted by significant quantities of landfill gas. In addition to 44 and 59 Clarke Avenue, four other properties had to be appropriately ventilated.

In view of the cause and effects of the catastrophic event, the local people asked for a public enquiry and the removal of the tip. Derbyshire County Council performed its own non-statutory enquiry which started in 1986, culminating in a public report in 1988.

Table 1.1 Typical gas analysis of landfill gas, the atmosphere and natural gas

GAS	LANDFILL GAS	NATURAL GAS	ATMOSPHERIC AIR
OXYGEN	1.8%	0.0%	21%
CARBON DIOXIDE	37%	0.3%	0.2%
NITROGEN	18%	1.8%	79%
HELIUM		TRACE	-
METHANE	54%	94%	-
METHANE/CARBON DIOXIDE	1.5:1	313:1	-
ETHANE	0.002%	3.25%	-
METHANE/ETHANE	27000:1	29:1	-

The report concluded that the explosion was indeed caused by the release and migration of landfill gas as a result of abnormal atmospheric conditions. A fall in atmospheric pressure of 35 *millibars* had been recorded in the 10 hours preceding the time of the explosion. The landfill site itself was insufficiently ventilated and so a system of induced ventilation needed to be established by means of holes bored for the collection and removal of the landfill gas. It was suggested that better co-ordination between the various authorities responsible for waste management should be implemented. A clear identification of those responsible for a site after it was no longer operational and the terms of that responsibility were both seen as being essential. The report also concluded that the potential environmental and public health problems associated with the complete removal of the tip were too great for this to be a viable solution. It also stated that refuse which was biodegradable could not properly be dumped on a landfill site close to domestic properties unless there was a thorough understanding of the site geology, and a rigorous application of appropriate methodology to ensure the satisfactory removal of landfill gas from the site. Clearly there had been a lot to learn from this incident about our past mistakes. Perhaps more consoling to the populace of Loscoe was the suggestion that the chance of a repetition of an explosion at the site was remote!

Although the Loscoe explosion stands out because of its disastrous consequences, surveys have shown that there are many other landfill sites which are potential sources of danger. In 1988, Her Majesty's Inspectorate of Pollution identified some 600 sites in the United Kingdom that needed the retrospective fitting of gas control methods. A further 700 sites near to domestic residences have been identified as potentially hazardous should gas migrate off site. Typically, the City of York in North Yorkshire has over 26 disused landfill sites within the city boundary. Indeed, in 1998, the York evening paper reported that action had to be taken to stop potentially dangerous methane gas from seeping from a former York rubbish tip towards a new housing estate.

The problem with older sites is that the waste content is totally unknown. The content is usually a mixture of both industrial and domestic wastes in varying proportions. If the surface of such a site were to be opened the result could well be a Pandora's Box containing a mixture of dangerous chemicals and other materials. In retrospect, it could be claimed that a more thoughtful approach to what should be have been placed in landfill sites and consideration of alternatives may well have prevented problems of the kind described here. The cautionary tale of Clarke Avenue would then have become a **precautionary** tale.

THE DYING SEA: OR HOW NOT TO MANAGE WATER RESOURCES.

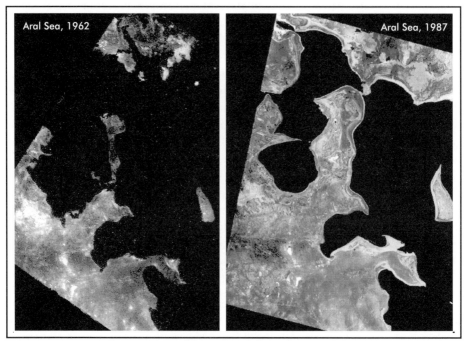

Figure 1.2 Aral Sea 1962 (left) and 1987 (right)

The Aral Sea is an inland sea situated in the Central Asian part of the old Soviet Union. It straddles south-western Kazakhstan and north-western Uzbekistan to the East of the Caspian Sea. For thousands of years it was the fourth largest inland sea in the world. There are two main tributary rivers called the Syr Darya and the Amu Darya. This sea is one of the world's most ancient and for centuries its size and depth remained essentially unchanged.

The sea was an important economical shipping route between the two chief ports and economic centres of Aralsk in the North and Muynak in the South. Annual catches from the Aral Sea of 45000 to 50000 tons of fish (sturgeon, perch, carp, etc.) were common. About a million muskrat pelts were taken from the surrounding area every year. There was a vast growth of reeds on its shores that supplied a large local paper making and packaging industry with its raw materials. Around a quarter of a million hectares of forest was found in the Amu Darya delta that gave passing shelter to migrant bird life and a home to some rare animals. The forest provided all year round pastures and a natural barrier to all forms of erosion.

Since the early 1960's the Aral Sea's volume has dropped by nearly 70%. This has halved the surface area and increased the *salinity* of its water to three times its original value, thus adversely affecting plant and animal life. The fishing industry is now almost non- existent and the waters are no longer transparent or filled with a wide variety of fish.

By early 1990 the loss of water from the sea was so severe that it became two bodies of water separated by a belt of dry land more than 100 metres wide at its narrowest point. The exposed sea bed is now covered by a white, alkaline soil. The southern Large Aral Sea is fed by the Amu Darya and the northern Small Aral Sea is fed by the Syr Darya. The area covered by the Aral Sea in 1974 was about 24635 square miles. In 1990 both seas covered a total area of about 14092 square miles. The volume of water in the sea has now become so reduced that current estimates indicate that it will no longer exist by 2010.

What caused such a dramatic and disastrous change? It was simply the improper use of a valuable natural resource by people.

In the early 1960's it was decided to grow and produce cotton in this region. Cotton requires a great deal of water and a huge canal irrigation system was built which drew water from both the Syr Darya and the Amu Darya. In the 1980's so much water was being taken from these rivers that not enough entered the Aral Sea to replace that lost by evaporation.

The high volumes of water taken for irrigation far exceeded what was necessary for the growing of cotton. These huge water losses were caused because of seepage from simple earthen irrigation channels before it ever reached cotton fields. The 1200km long Karakum Canal, which takes its water from the Amu Darya, runs in direct contact with loose desert sands for hundreds of kilometres. This has created a 800km^2 "sea" along this canal in Turkmenia. In villages alongside the canal, water has found its way into the cellars, communication lines have been cut, and buildings have collapsed because the ground underneath has sunk. Trees in valley areas have become waterlogged with the subsequent loss of orchards and vineyards. To protect the city of Ashkhabad, which is now surrounded by marshlands, a number of wells have had to be dug to enable water drainage. A reservoir (Maryysk Oblast, Turkmenia) built in the middle of a desert was not properly prepared to hold water. The water seeps into the ground as if through a sieve. Because of the wasteful way in which the water is transported, it has been estimated that two to four times the normal volume of water is used to produce the cotton.

There has also been other far-reaching damage. Water lost by seepage from transport canals, irrigation canals, reservoirs, and by the careless disposal of collected and drained water from agricultural fields has been added to the water table in many areas. This groundwater is saturated with minerals, particularly salt. In places the added water has caused the groundwater to rise to the surface, bringing with it its dissolved salt. The salt has contaminated agricultural land and has prevented the growth of crops. The scale of the problem is shown by the fact that nearly 40% of irrigated land in Turkmenistan is subject to this secondary salination. In Turkmenia the annual rate of land loss due to salination now exceeds the rate at which new land is brought into agricultural use.

In the autumn and winter, after the cotton is harvested, attempts are made to desalinate the soil by flushing it with "new" water at least four times before replanting. If this were not done crops would not be able to grow. Unfortunately, washing away the salt also removes many other soluble minerals vital for plant growth and therefore the fertility of the soil is reduced. Much more fertiliser is then used than would otherwise be necessary.

The water drained from irrigated fields in the middle and upper reaches of the Amu Darya thus contains a high concentration of dissolved salts which have been deposited miles away in low lying areas. This drainage water has collected in natural depressions where it has formed unwelcome saline lakes. Again it has been added to groundwater, spoiling its quality, and turning pasture land into marshland. Salt-saturated water, together with untreated domestic and industrial waste, has also been dumped into the irrigation canals and the Amu Darya. The result of this is that both drinking water and agricultural land have been badly polluted.

In some areas the water-borne pollution of soil has also been augmented by the deposit of harmful dusts brought by winds from the dying Aral Sea. Soils have thus accumulated a wide variety of potentially harmful substances such as pesticides, mineral fertilisers, *nitrites* and *nitrates*, which have found their way into the human food chain. In addition to this, the exhaustion of soil caused by the over-cropping of cotton has occurred in the traditionally very productive region of Uzabek. This has been accompanied by an increase in plant diseases and pests, which has resulted in the application of mineral fertilisers and pesticides. This in turn has caused the death of much of the soil fauna and yet again the pollution of local water supplies.

The consequences of all of this pollution have been dire. Whilst it is often difficult to prove conclusively that there are links between pollution levels and medical conditions, investigations have shown an undoubted increase in various illnesses and diseases. Research carried out in Ashkhabad Oblast shows a possible relationship between organic pesticides and gall bladder, liver and pancreatic diseases. Mineral pesticides have been linked to psychiatric disorders and premature births. Turkmenia has a very high infant mortality rate and very frequent outbreaks of intestinal disorders. These again have been linked to the use of water drawn from the heavily contaminated Amu Darya for drinking purposes. The water can also contain a high concentration of bacteria, which appears to be linked to the occurrence of typhoid cases eight times greater than the national average for Russia. In the lower reaches of the Amu Darya, water is so unsuitable for drinking, even after boiling, that it threatens the lives and health of nearly three million people. In the Uzabek region, yellow jaundice and intestinal diseases have resulted in a soaring death rate, especially amongst children. In the vicinity of the Aral Sea the levels of kidney and liver diseases are high, and in some areas the infant mortality rate is as high as 1 in 10. Cancer of the oesophagus is one of the most widespread diseases, with hepatitis and gastric diseases being common. About 40% of the Kazakh Republic's cases of epidemic jaundice occur in Kzyl Ordinisk Oblast alone. Perhaps the most poignant point of all is that in some areas, nursing mothers have been advised not to breast feed their babies because their milk has been found to be toxic.

There are also major concerns that the reduction in size of the Aral Sea is affecting the weather patterns of neighbouring regions. However, as in the medical cases, it is difficult to prove conclusively. What is clear is that the reduction in size has been paralleled by serious changes in local daily seasonal temperatures. A temperature variation now exists which is threatening the production of cotton.

Since the surface area of the Aral Sea has been greatly reduced, the initially dry winds that blow over the sea no longer carry the same amount of water as in previous years. This may reduce snow falls in the mountains to the south and seems to be related to dust storms occurring in places in Central Asia where they didn't occur before.

Finally, the wet lands associated with the sea itself have nearly all dried up. The reed beds have gone, together with about 80% of the forest. Of the 178 species of animals previously found in the delta of the Amu Darya only 38 remain.

This wanton destruction of a valuable natural resource need not and should not have happened. Attention was paid to some of the possible consequences but the authorities prevailing at that time were even willing to accept the total loss of this sea. The relatively cheap proper engineering and regulation of the water irrigation system would have prevented the wastage of water. To put things right now would be very costly and an immense technical challenge.

Just in Case You're not Convinced.......

There are, of course, many more examples we could have used to illustrate the problems involved in managing resources. We hope that by now you're thoroughly convinced that this is an area which needs urgent attention. For those of you who are not, here are one or two more illustrations of how the misuse of natural and man-made resources has led to their loss, the pollution of the environment and serious damage to living organisms at all levels.

In the 1950's and 1960's, Japan's emerging industries belched out millions of tonnes of dangerous pollutants into its waterways and atmosphere. One episode in particular resulted in horrific damage to some of the people of Minimata on the island of Kyushu. Here a factory allowed *mercury* compounds to pollute a local bay. Mercury thus entered the food chain via fish that were then caught and eaten by the local population. Thousands of people developed neurological disorders, leaving them unable to co-ordinate their movements or crippled completely. Many children were born with severe physical deformities and mental disabilities. Disasters such as this have resulted in Japan becoming one of the most environmentally conscious countries in the world today.

In India there are about 170 million people, living in a 100km wide belt along a coastline of about 6100km, who are directly or indirectly dependent on the coastal ecosystem. Every year, about 40 km^3 of sewage and industrial wastes are put into the seas around India together with about 50 million cubic metres of solid waste. If agricultural wastes, silt, etc., and the oil pollution caused by intensive shipping of oil, refinery wastes and harbour activities are also included, it can be seen why many Indian people are so concerned about the state of their seas. In Madras alone some 3000 tonnes of garbage are produced every day. About one-third of the population live in slums and have no access to services such as sanitation and solid waste management. Large numbers of livestock also add to the sanitary and waste disposal problems. Many households generally recycle paper products, glass, metal and plastics. Hence both the organic and moisture contents of the garbage are high. This causes a problem with regard to disposal because such material has a low calorific value and cannot be easily burned. Thus it is not suitable for energy recovery. Indeed, resource recovery plants in India generally have failed to treat garbage successfully. The garbage of Madras is taken away by road and dumped in low-lying areas as landfill. Unfortunately, modern landfill practice is not carried out. This has resulted in unsanitary sites that are infested with disease carrying organisms, flies, pigs and other living things. These sites have on occasions contaminated nearby ground water, and caused the loss of coastal and other wetlands.

So what can be done, and where do you fit in?

You may well have found the details in this chapter depressing and worrying. However, all of the situations described are ones from which we can learn - history can teach us lessons, albeit severe ones. From these past experiences people have begun to realise that the Earth's resources are not endless and there is a limit to what is available for use. The improper management of resources can lead to their non-availability for future generations and have serious environmental effects on all living organisms.

Fortunately the news is not all bad news. In many industrialised countries attempts are being made to adopt more logical management procedures in large scale manufacturing and other processes to maximise the use of resources, eliminate excess waste and dispose of waste, in ways that minimise environmental effects. This has to be done whilst still meeting people's needs for better products and/or lower costs (more value). Many companies producing goods or services in response to our needs are adopting this "more value for less resource usage and waste" approach coupled with a careful assessment of waste production and disposal from "cradle to grave". At an individual level, you can support this by a more careful, thoughtful approach in your use of materials; by not producing excessive waste, and by adopting a positive attitude to the recovery of waste. If this were done throughout your country by everyone, just think of what could be saved and recovered. It should be pointed out, however, that there are no easy answers to the complex and vast problems associated with the use of resources and its consequences. It must be remembered that no process can ever be free of waste production.

Approaches to dealing with waste have changed from purely financial considerations (i.e. waste means a loss in money), to those that rely on laws and regulations (i.e. legislation). There are two basic legislative tools that are in operation - the so-called "end-of-pipe" regulations and the "strategic targets" approach.

As the name suggests, "end-of-pipe" means taking action when the waste has been produced. Here the regulations are technical in nature and relate to particular processes in waste treatment and disposal, e.g. emission control regulations for incinerators. Many such regulations have been "add-ons" in that they have grown out of experience and have evolved as the problems associated with waste production and disposal have become evident, i.e. the measures taken have been retrospective in nature. Such regulations have been designed to ensure the safe operation of waste disposal processes, and operate as a "fine tuning" for a particular system by promoting the use of the best technology practices available. They have **not**, however, led to major changes in the way waste management systems operate. Such changes will be produced by planning an approach which combines different waste management procedures rather than the refining of the procedures themselves. You can help to influence regulations by becoming more scientifically and technically literate so that you can understand the problems involved and argue from a more informed position. In addition, the individual's support for those agencies which recognise the need for law/regulation introduction and enforcement in the protection of the environment is paramount. You can complain, report and act as an "environmental watchdog" within a legal framework. Public pressure has been a powerful political tool and has influenced legislation in many instances.

A "strategic targets" approach is being used increasingly in the UK and abroad to define ways in which all types of wastes will be dealt with in future. The legislation here is based on a "hierarchy of waste management" and sets targets for the recovery and recycling of waste in a kind of order. This order is headed by **source reduction**, i.e. waste minimisation. This might then, for example in the case of solid waste, be followed by re-use, recycling, composting, conversion of waste to energy, incineration without energy recovery and landfill, in some order of preference. You can of course minimise your own waste production and make decisions about how some of your waste can be reused and recycled. However, even this approach may not necessarily result in the lowest of environmental impacts nor in achieving economical results in financial terms. Cost in particular has been a major problem in trying to relieve the effects of waste management on the environment. Two concepts are becoming established which will help to overcome fears concerning the costs involved. The first takes into account the legislation requiring the limitation of waste emissions and therefore costs are examined at the site from where the waste originates. The second idea allows for the building of any environmental objectives into the waste management system from the very start of a process rather than, more expensively, bolting them on at a later stage.

A possible approach that will help even further is advocated in the following chapters. It is one based on "Prevention is better than cure", involving the integration of a wide variety of waste disposal methods and recycling. It is referred to as the "**Integrated Waste Management**". Its basis lies in the concept of "**sustainable development**" which has been defined as "meeting the needs of the current generation without compromising the ability of future generations to meet their own needs". Clearly there is a need to work out a programme that minimises waste production and maximises the use of the available resources before a project or the manufacture of a product is started. If this work were to be done first the effects on the environment would be considerable. Certainly the careful control of waste production and its disposal will result in a reduction in the amount of pollutants making their way back into the environment. A well-managed approach to the use of materials and waste production will help to ensure that the resources available now will still be available for the next generation. The best way of ensuring this is to appreciate that different materials in any waste stream are best dealt with by different processes, so to deal with the whole waste stream a range of management options is needed (a lateral system). If real and sustained environmental improvements are the objectives then a single, integrated collection and sorting system followed by a material-specific recovery/treatment/disposal of waste represents the most promising way forward. Indeed, such an approach will enable a proper assessment of overall environmental impacts and economic costs. The following chapters set out to explore this approach.

Some industries in the developed countries seem set on a course which is designed to improve resource management. At a more personal level, it may be that you cannot directly influence people's attitudes towards resource management in other countries or indeed your own, but that does not stop you from doing your best to set a good example in the way you manage your waste, nor from being an advocate for the efficient usage of our world's resources and the protection of the environment. A collective effort by all like-thinking people can force the changes necessary to prevent the environmental fears that the present generations have for those who come after us.

FACT FILE 1.1
The nature and origin of methane - a chemical interlude.

Pure methane is a colourless, odourless, tasteless gas. It is a hydrocarbon in that it contains only the elements carbon and hydrogen. Its chemical formula is CH_4. It has a lower explosive limit (LEL) of 5.3% by volume with air. This means, for example, that $100m^3$ of a mixture of air and methane containing $94.7m^3$ of air and $5.3m^3$ of methane would be an explosive combination. Its upper explosion limit (UEL) is 15.0% by volume with air. It is therefore a very serious fire and explosion hazard when exposed to a source of heat.

Methane is probably best known as the major component of North Sea (Natural) gas. For domestic use this is mixed with a special chemical to give it a characteristic smell for safety reasons. It is also trapped in coal seams and is often released during the mining of coal - here it is known as fire-damp and has been the cause of many deep mine explosions.

In landfill sites, methane is produced by the decomposition of the biodegradable materials some metres below the surface of the landfill site. The actual composition and rate of emission of this "landfill gas" are variable and depend on the composition of the materials contained within the site, compaction, and surface and underground treatments of the dumped waste. Some materials, however, can remain unchanged for decades.

Domestic waste consists mainly of paper, wood, food, plastics, metal, glass and textiles in varying proportions. The organic constituents in this waste are broken down by natural bacterial action in two stages. In the first stage *carbohydrates* (e.g. paper), *proteins* (e.g. meat, fish) and *fats* are broken down into simple *sugars*, *amino acids*, *glycerol* and long chain *fatty acids* respectively. This is then followed by the production of carbon dioxide, hydrogen and short chain fatty acids that lead to the second stage production of methane and more carbon dioxide. A typical composition by volume of landfill gas is given in Table 1.1. The compositions of normal air and of natural gas are also given for comparative purposes.

Apart from the material present there are five external factors that effect the production of landfill gas. Firstly, an increase in water content of the waste material is paralleled by an increase in the rate of decomposition and therefore gas generation. Secondly, *pH* or how acidic the landfill material is dictates the survival of the methane producing bacteria, the optimum pH range lying between 6.4 and 7.4. The third factor is temperature, which should lie between 29C and 37C for the existence of successful anaerobic digestion conditions. Core landfill temperatures are well within this range of temperatures. The presence or absence of oxygen is the fourth factor. As gas leaves the landfill site, it is replaced by air, particularly in the surface area. Oxygen in this air is toxic to *anaerobic* bacteria and hence it inhibits the production of methane. Thus the depth of the site, the rate of gas extraction and the permeability of the covering material are all important. The last factor is time. There is no set time pattern but typically a steady rate of production of gas, containing 55-65% volume for volume of methane, is achieved in one to two years.

FACT FILE 1.2
Organic Materials - another chemical interlude.

Many of the substances mentioned in this chapter are organic chemicals, i.e. compounds which contain the element carbon (C). There are several million different compounds of carbon, both man-made and natural, currently known. The study of such compounds is called organic chemistry. Carbon has the almost unique ability to bond repeatedly with itself to form chains and rings of atoms. This means that it is able to form compounds with molecular structures of considerable complexity. It is predominantly the element of life, forming the backbone of such compounds as carbohydrates, proteins and fats. Synthetic chemicals based on carbon include plastics, dyes, rubbers and medicinal compounds. Elements commonly found bonded to carbon in these compounds are hydrogen (H), oxygen (O) and nitrogen (N), and to a lesser extent sulphur (S), phosphorus (P), chlorine (Cl), bromine (Br) and fluorine (F). In fact the range of elements carbon can combine with is extensive and includes the metallic elements. This latter area of chemistry is called organo-metallic chemistry.

To illustrate the above we will examine the chemicals known as carbohydrates. These are chemical substances made of the elements carbon, hydrogen and oxygen. Carbohydrates, like many other carbon based compounds, are made by living things, which is the reason why these compounds have been given the generic name of organic chemicals. They are a constituent of food. The simplest carbohydrates are the sugars, usually with five or six carbon atoms in each molecule. Glucose and fructose are two naturally occurring sugars. These sugars have the same formula, $C_6H_{12}O_6$, but different structures. One molecule of each combines with the loss of water to make cane sugar (sucrose, $C_{12}H_{22}O_{11}$) which occurs in sugarcane and sugar-beet. Starch and cellulose are carbohydrates consisting of hundreds of glucose molecules linked together. Note that whatever name has been given to the above compounds they are all organic or carbon-based in nature.

Further Reading: Chapter 1

N.V. Aladin, *Ecological State of the Fauna of the Aral Sea During the Last 30 Years*, GeoJournal, 1995, **35**, No.1

P.Appasamy & J. Lundqvist, *Water Supply & Waste Disposal Strategies for Madras*, Ambio, November, 1993, **22**, No.7

W.S.Ellis & D.Turner, *A Soviet Sea Lies Dying*, National Geographic, 1990, **177**, No.2

A.Levintanus, *On the Fate of the Aral Sea*, Environments,1993, **22**, No.1

P.P. Micklin, *The Shrinking Aral Sea*, Geotimes,1993, **38**, No.4

R.Milne, *Methane Menace Seeps to the Surface*, New Scientist, 1988, **117**, No.1601

F.Pearce, *Poisoned Waters; The Aral Sea has all but vanished, but its legacy is destroying the health of more than a million people*, New Scientist, 1995, **148**, No. 2000

J. Perera, *A Sea Turns to Dust*, New Scientist, 1993, **140**, No.1896

N.Precoda, *Requiem for the Aral Sea*, Ambio, 1991, **20**, No.3-4

W.Rathje & C.Murphy, *Rubbish! The Archaeology of Garbage: What Our Garbage Tells Us About Ourselves*, New York, Harper Collins Publishers, 1992

K.M.Richards, *A Modern Fuel from an Age Old Process - Landfill Gas*, National Society for Clean Air 55th Annual Conference, 1988

R.Sloof, *The Dying Aral Sea*, World Health; The Magazine of the World Health Organisation, July, 1992.

Technical Advisory Working Party, *Report on Methane Generation from Landfill Sites*, Warwickshire Environmental Protection Council, 1988

P.Young. *Expertise or Explosions - Landfill Gas, the Role of the Consultant*, Environmental Health, 1989, **97**, No.7

G.V.Voropaev, *Can the Aral Sea be Recovered Today?*, Water Resources, 1993, **19**, No.2

CHAPTER 2

ENVIRONMENTAL RISK AND SAFETY
an asian war and an asbestos factory

Asbestos and dioxins are used to show the damaging effects that human activities can have on people and their environment. Explanations given include: how a hazard is identified, the meaning of dose-response relationship, how exposure levels are determined and how risk characterisation is carried out. The importance of managing risk is emphasised, together with the fact that all human activities entail balancing risk with benefit.

A SOUTH-EAST ASIAN WAR

In January 1962, at the start of the USA involvement in what became known as the Vietnam War, a programme was initiated which was to raise a very heated controversy concerning the use of chemicals on the environment which continues to this day. Under the programme named "Ranch Hand", US forces used aircraft to spray selected areas of jungle with large amounts of defoliating agents. The job of these _herbicide_ chemicals was to strip the leaves off trees, thus denying the enemy (the Viet Cong) the use of the jungle as a hiding place. This programme of defoliation proved, in the end, not to be very successful.

The major material used was code named _Agent Orange_ (see Fact File 2.1) and was thought to contain two herbicides. Unfortunately, depending upon the source and the degree of control during the manufacture of the herbicides, Agent Orange was later found to be contaminated with chemicals known as _dioxins_ (levels ranging from $2-50\mu g/g$). Although there are no precise figures available it is widely believed that these dioxins caused innumerable animal deaths. In addition, because of both the deliberate and accidental delivery of Agent Orange to agricultural land, dioxins have been blamed for the increase in prenatal deaths and in the birth of deformed Vietnamese children. Such was the outcry both nationally and internationally that in 1969 the National Institute of Health (USA) investigated the use of Agent Orange. As a consequence of this investigation, the last mission was flown in May 1970. The USA had come perilously close to being accused of chemical warfare!

After the Vietnam War USA veterans who had been exposed to Agent Orange claimed that the illnesses they have experienced, including cancer and genetic disorders in their children, were caused by the presence of dioxins.

ARMLEY, LEEDS, UK

In 1993 at Armley in the City of Leeds, England, the death of some 180 men and women, which had occurred over a period of 16 years, was investigated by a team of lawyers from Manhattan, USA. These deaths were linked to a local _asbestos_ (see Fact File 2.2) factory that had closed down in 1958. All of the dead had either worked at this factory or had relatives who had worked there. All had suffered from a form of malignant cancer known as _mesothelioma_ (see Fact File 2.3) which is uniquely associated with asbestos.

The inhalation of even a minute amount of asbestos can kill, and for years the deadly dust from the Armley factory had been a fact of local life. Shortly before his death in 1988 at the age of 42 one victim of mesothelioma recalled how his mother came home from working at the factory covered with asbestos dust - he believed he had developed the cancer by playing with his mother's coat as a small boy. Yet another victim who died in 1990 at the age of 43 recalled how as a boy he had licked

Figure 2.1 Aircraft in formation spraying the jungle in Vietnam with defoliating agent

his fingers after writing his name in the asbestos dust on the pavements outside his home. Neither of these victims ever worked at the factory!

By 1993, out of 290 inhabited houses checked for asbestos pollution in the immediate vicinity of the closed factory, 258 needed to be evacuated and decontaminated. The factory itself was left in a badly contaminated form with asbestos dust and other debris still lying about both inside the buildings and in the surrounding yard. It appeared that every nook and cranny had asbestos fibres in it.

The factory at Armley in Leeds started as a family business in 1870 making asbestos mattresses for lagging steam engines. In 1921 it was merged with another company to form the world's biggest and most powerful asbestos company. This new company ran 15 factories in the UK plus huge asbestos mines in Canada, South Africa, and what was then Rhodesia. It also operated factories in India and the USA. The technique which made this company particularly famous was developed from an Armley idea in 1931. This involved mixing raw asbestos with water and cement which could then be sprayed onto a surface requiring insulation. The technique was portable and cheap, and almost any surface could be sprayed to provide instant sound proofing and fire proofing. Asbestos thus became a component of thousands of public buildings such as hospitals, schools and theatres, spread throughout the world. It was such a coating, sprayed onto a large USA Manhattan bank, which brought the American lawyers to the UK. The coating, containing brown asbestos, had visibly begun to disintegrate, thus posing a hazard to the bank's work force.

What are the factors which link a war that finished in 1975 in South-East Asia and an area of Leeds in the UK in the 1990's? The answer to this question lies in an examination of such terms as pollution, hazard, risk, risk assessment and risk management.

ENVIRONMENTAL POLLUTION

Most people think in terms of the effects of pollution when considering environmental risk and safety. Environmental pollution can be described as being the discharge of any material (e.g. dioxins, asbestos) or energy into the *biosphere* which may cause short term (acute) or long term (chronic) damage to the Earth's ecological balance, or which lowers the quality of life. Pollutants may cause damage which is immediate and easily identifiable, or damage of an insidious nature which is only detectable over a long period of time.

Increases in world-wide industrialisation, transport systems and population have caused very rapid increases in the production of both material goods and services. This has resulted in a very large increase in the use of natural resources and in the production of waste materials. The indiscriminate discharge of untreated industrial and domestic wastes into the biosphere, the "throwaway" attitude towards solid wastes in particular, and the use of chemicals without considering the potential consequences, have resulted in major environmental disasters.

Public worries about the production of waste and the use of chemicals seem to lie in six main areas. These are
- the exposure of human beings to toxic materials which can cause living cells to mutate more rapidly, physical abnormalities in a developing embryo or foetus, the formation of cancers, and other slow latent effects on health;
- the tipping of waste leading to the acute poisoning of living organisms;
- the contamination of ground water;
- the marring or destruction of amenities because of the presence of waste or hazardous materials;
- the irreversible damage caused by the disposal of long-lived pollutants on land or at sea;
- the waste of resources which could be recovered from so-called rubbish.

How can pollution be controlled so that the effects of pollutants on people and the environment are minimised? There are four general approaches which can be adopted to control pollution. The first is to temporarily stop or reduce the output from a process which is producing a high degree of pollution. This would only allow short-term respite for the environment. The second method involves the dispersal, and hence the dilution, of pollutants. An example of this might be the use of taller chimney stacks which would certainly reduce effects on a local population but not on communities further away. We are all familiar with acid rain and its suggested consequences in Scandinavian countries caused in part, it is believed, by the burning of fossil fuels in the UK (see Chapter 8). The third method is to remove the pollutants produced during a process before they are emitted to air and water. Unfortunately, such pollutants may need to be treated before being buried or stored on land where they can again pose a potential hazard. The last method entails the **changing** of a process to reduce pollution. This can involve the production of lower amounts of pollutants because the process has been improved, the substitution of a less hazardous material, or the separation and reuse of materials from the waste stream. Changing an industrial process is considered by many to be the most effective and efficient way to meet the demands being made to control waste and minimise natural resource use, and to meet the increase in costs of pollution control, waste disposal and raw materials.

RISK ASSESSMENT

Risk assessment attempts to identify the hazards and risks involved in a particular process or activity and to determine ways of managing those hazards and risks. A **hazard** is simply a substance, process or activity which has the potential to cause harm. In the context of the environment, **risk** may be defined as the likelihood of suffering a harmful effect or effects resulting from exposure to some chemical, biological or physical agent. Risk is usually expressed in terms of the probability of an adverse effect occurring.

In the past, it has been relatively simple to identify a hazard and to devise ways of dealing with it based on common sense. In every home there is always the risk of a fire hazard. Our response to this risk has been based on previous experience in that we know what commonly causes a fire, e.g. unswept chimneys, faulty electrical devices such as washing machines, smoking in bed. Hence we try to avoid a fire in our home by having the chimney swept, ensuring that electrical safety codes are properly followed, and not smoking in bed! We try to lessen the possible outcome of a fire by identifying escape routes, fitting smoke alarms, acquiring knowledge about the best ways of tackling a fire, and by establishing a fire brigade service. All of this has evolved over a period of time without the need to resort to elaborate calculations or analytical techniques. However, when you take out a fire insurance policy the company you deal with will have assessed the risk of a fire hazard. This takes into account such things as how often house fires occur, how big claims tend to be, the age of the property, the district you live in, previous fire accident claims and so on. In other words, if the risk is to be properly assessed, many factors have to be taken into account, including the size of the event and the magnitude of the population exposed. Risk therefore depends on both the probability of an event occurring and the severity of the event should it occur.

The evolutionary approach to risk assessment becomes less useful the more complex a system becomes. Indeed, a more rigid and mathematically based approach to risk assessment is developing because many man-made systems are so complex that it is not possible for one single person to understand the whole system. Risk assessment attempts to quantify the probabilities and degrees of harm that result from a complex operation. It is not so easy to define risk assessment because of the wide range of situations in which it used. For example, the US Environmental Protection Agency sees risk assessment as the process which clearly identifies the potential safety and health effects caused by the exposure of individuals and populations to hazardous materials and situations. It has also been defined as the identification of hazards and their causes, the estimation of probability that harm will result and the balancing of harm with any resulting benefit.

Risk assessment is done so that intelligent management decisions can be made concerning the health and welfare of all living things, to understand and improve existing technology design, to educate people so they can make informed decisions, and to improve the economic and social welfare of people.

HOW IS RISK ASSESSMENT DONE?

There are many methods of risk assessment, but most of them contain four essential elements: hazard identification, establishment of a dose-response relationship, determination of exposure levels, and risk characterisation.

Hazard identification

This is the vital first step because if any hazards are missed out in the risk assessment then it will have been carried out on the wrong basis. The basis for the identification of a hazard, whether it be biological, chemical or physical in nature, lies in the examination of statistical data collected from a large population of humans which has experienced the hazard, or by the direct testing of the agent on appropriate living organisms. Hazard identification is a qualitative process which often involves the use of a range of techniques to identify the hazard, and is a complex procedure.

Were the hazards correctly identified in the cases of Agent Orange and asbestos? Let us answer this question by first reviewing the evidence concerning the dioxins and then that for asbestos.

Dioxins

By the late 1960's scientists had become aware of the presence of dangerous by-products called dioxins in certain herbicides, particularly those containing or derived from a chemical we will label simply TCP. Several accidental exposures of large groups of people to substances containing dioxins led to their investigation as hazardous chemicals.

One of the earliest accidents occurred in 1949. A container used for the production of TCP at the Monsanto plant in West Virginia, USA, blew up. This exposed workers to TCP, and these workers were then affected by chloracne, a severe and persistent form of acne which can lead to permanent disfigurement. The cause of this was later identified to be the presence of a dioxin known as TCDD in the reaction mixture.

In November 1953 a runaway chemical reaction at BASF's Ludwigshafen plant in West Germany caused a vat containing TCP contaminated with TCDD to boil over. Hundreds of workers were contaminated, some developing chloracne. Since so many workers had been affected, here was an ideal opportunity to study a large sample. Unfortunately, West German legislation worked against the acquisition of *epidemiological* information and thus the possibility of a useful risk assessment was lost. The medical histories of the victims, which were held by West Germany's state-run health insurance companies, were not available due to the enforcement of strict data protection law. In 1990 the law changed and access to some data allowed, providing that no individual was identified. Research so far has shown an 18% increase in general illness for the exposed workers compared with a *control group*. In particular there has been a dramatic increase in thyroid diseases, intestinal and respiratory infections and disorders of the peripheral nervous system. There has been no increase in illness from cancer. It would appear from this German study that dioxins disturb the human *immune system* and *hormonal* control mechanisms.

Since 1979 in the USA there has been a federal ban which has eliminated some uses of herbicides containing TCP. North American studies have shown dioxins to be present in many industrial wastes, paper-mill effluents being a notorious example. Areas around some chemical plants are heavily contaminated and dioxins have been found in parts of the Great Lakes. Dioxins have also entered the environment through the use of contaminated oil as a roadway dust suppressant, so much so that the town of Times Beach, Montana, was abandoned in 1983 because tests indicated that highway spraying had left high levels of dioxins in the soil.

It would appear, then, that in dioxins we have serious chemical pollutants.

Could the hazards with Agent Orange and the other examples have been identified much earlier? Are they examples of ignorance, lack of scientific investigation, or indifference?

Asbestos

The problem for asbestos victims is the length of time it takes for the disease to become evident, so that claims for compensation have proved to be difficult to bring to court. Indeed, many victims have died whilst waiting for their cases to be considered. This is because companies such as the one involved at Armley, against which complaints have been made, have claimed ignorance of the effects of asbestos, and because much of the damage was caused before legislation controlling the use of asbestos was in place. In other words it has been claimed that proper hazard identification, risk assessment procedures and control mechanisms did not exist. What is the truth behind this?

The first recognition of the dangers of asbestos dates back to a Factory Inspector's report of 1898, with the first recorded asbestos related death of a male aged 33 years recorded in 1900. Further investigations showed that ten other asbestos workers, all aged about 30 years, had died prior to 1900. So one could say there was strong evidence that something was not quite right about asbestos nearly 100 years ago. In 1929, a pathologist at Leeds University made a study of the lungs of asbestos workers at Armley. He noted the presence of asbestos fibres not only in the workers themselves but also in the lungs of a man who had never worked at the factory. This was perhaps the first recorded case of an environmental exposure. In 1931 the UK Government passed the Asbestos Industry Regulations to control dust in the workplace. In 1935 the first cases of asbestos related lung cancer were reported. In 1943, the company owning the factory at Armley, together with other asbestos companies, sponsored research into the health effects of asbestos. This research used white mice and showed that 81% of the mice that inhaled long fibre asbestos developed lung cancer. In 1955 a further study of the lung cancer rates amongst this company's workers showed it was ten times the national average. The real turning point came in the late 1950's when a South African physician discovered 33 cancer related deaths in a blue asbestos mining community in the Transvaal. Their findings were published in 1960 and showed that mesothelioma tumours were killing both the miners and people who had never worked with asbestos. In the USA a 1961 study of World War II shipyard workers demonstrated the connection between airborne asbestos and the development of disease 20 or more years after exposure, and indicated that it was probable that the asbestos industry knew of the dangers far earlier.

As a consequence of the acceptance of asbestos as a serious health hazard, from 1969 until the present time protective regulations and laws have been passed in the UK. The use of asbestos and the modification of buildings and other structures involving asbestos have become so strictly controlled that only license holders can work with asbestos. The import, supply and use of the two most dangerous forms, blue and brown asbestos, are prohibited, and the prohibition extends to second hand materials. The use of white asbestos, which is claimed to be less dangerous, is also strictly limited. All aspects of asbestos manufacture, processing, repairing, maintenance, construction, demolition, removal and disposal are now covered by legal requirements and rigorously enforced in the UK.

Establishment of the Dose-Response Relationship

The dose-response assessment involves the determination of the relationship between the dose of an agent administered or received and the incidence of an adverse health effect in exposed populations. Again this relatively simple definition hides the need to appreciate the range of factors that should be taken into account, e.g. age range of the population, gender, level of exposure, length of time of exposure.

The relationship between dose and response is established by testing the agent through bioassays and epidemiological studies. A bioassay involves the assessment of the strength and effect of an agent by testing it on living organisms and comparing the results with those determined for another agent. Epidemiology is the study of disease in a human population, defining its incidence and prevalence, examining the role of external influences such as infection, diet or other toxic substances and examining appropriate preventative or creative measures. Such information is not always available for every hazard and the study of human exposure is not always practical or ethical. The presence of external factors, in particular, makes it very difficult to establish a link between cause and effect. In order to surmount these problems the effect of exposure of animals to hazards is used. The validity of data based on animal experimentation in order to establish human dose-response relationships is a subject of heated debate. This includes ethical considerations as well as the more scientifically based ones concerning the validity of extrapolation from high to low doses and from animal data to humans.

To date, TCDD and other dioxins have been definitely proved to cause only one disease in humans, and that is chloracne. Concerns about dioxin are largely based on the very small amounts required to produce birth defects and deaths in small mammals (see Table 2.1). It is because of the lethal effect of TCDD on animals that some scientists believe dioxins to be amongst the most poisonous chemicals made by man. Other effects of dioxins on humans are still not yet proven although they are suspected of causing miscarriages, birth defects and serious behavioural and neurological problems.

In the case of asbestos, the 1985 Asbestos (Licensing) Regulation noted that "there was no safe level of asbestos".

Table 2.1. Lethal Dose of TCCD in Different Species

ANIMAL	$LD_{50}(\mu g/kg\ bw)^*$	ANIMAL	$LD_{50}(\mu g/kg\ bw)^*$
Guinea pig	1	Rat(male)	22
Rat(female)	45	Monkey	<70
Rabbit	115	Mouse	114
Dog	>300	Bullfrog	>500
Hamster	5000	-	-

*LD_{50}: the dose that causes 50% of the sample to die.
$\mu g/kg$ bw: micrograms per kilogram body weight

Determination of Exposure Levels

This is a very vital stage in risk assessment. It involves identifying those exposed to the hazard; evaluating their susceptibility; evaluating the route of entry of the hazard; and the magnitude, frequency and duration of exposure.

Identifying and describing the population at risk often requires a long and in-depth study. This is because of the many factors that determine the extent to which a hazard will affect a particular population, e.g. occupation, living and working conditions, place of residence, state of health, gender and age.

Risk Characterisation

Risk characterisation is the estimation of the size of a public health problem. This evaluation is determined by combining the information on the dose-response relationship and the exposure assessment. Any inherent uncertainties encompassed in the risk assessment should be specified when characterising the risk.

For example, in 1994 the USA Environmental Protection Agency (EPA) reported that an unknown number of Americans had been exposed to levels of dioxins that may impair their immune system. This Agency identified the biggest source of exposure for people to be contaminated food. Dioxins are not taken up by plants but can enter the food chain by deposition on leaves which are then eaten by herbivores. It is suggested that dioxins cause between 1 in 1000 and 1 in 10000 cancers in the USA. This report has led to extensive debate since the EPA has suggested such a small upper limit (0.006 pg of dioxins per day for each kilogram of a person's body weight) that it would be exceeded by natural deposits provided by volcanoes and wood burning fires.

In the USA, the EPA has estimated that 3,000 to 12,000 cases of cancer, usually fatal, are caused annually in the United States by asbestos exposure. In 1971 asbestos became the first material to be regulated by the USA Occupational Safety and Health Administration (OSHA). In 1986, OSHA drastically reduced work-exposure levels. In 1989, the EPA ordered that the manufacture, use, and export of asbestos be reduced by 94 percent over a 7-year period. The order thus ended the use of asbestos for all building materials and for brake linings. Controversy continues to surround the EPA's assessment of asbestos insulation as a strong health hazard. In 1991, the USA Appeals Court ruled that *"..it did not believe that spending $200-300 million to save approximately 7 lives over 13 years was reasonable..", "... risks were overshadowed by one death a year from ingested toothpicks...", "...hazards had not been considered from alternatives to asbestos..", and "..insufficient evidence had been produced to substantiate a ban ...".* Critics also maintain that chrysotile asbestos, unlike the amphibole form, is not a health hazard in the workplace.

In the UK in 1994 The Health and Safety Executive published its position statement on asbestos. It stated that asbestos is responsible for more occupation-related deaths than any other single cause. One asbestos-related disease, mesothelioma, is currently responsible for more than 1000 people dying each year in the UK. Virtually all these deaths are associated with exposure to asbestos. The other major fatal disease linked to asbestos is lung cancer. It is estimated that for every death due to mesothelioma, there are two deaths from asbestos-induced lung cancer.

Together with the other serious asbestos-related disease, asbestosis, it is estimated that asbestos is currently responsible for between 3000-3500 deaths annually. The number of deaths is likely to continue to rise probably until 2010 and possibly to 2025. If nothing changes, it is expected that the number of asbestos-related deaths may eventually peak somewhere between 5000 and 10000 annually. It is clear that because of the long period of time before asbestos related diseases manifest themselves, the deaths now occurring and those expected to occur in the near future reflect industrial practices of the past rather than the effectiveness of current law and work practices. The effectiveness of regulation has yet to be demonstrated.

The case against dioxins is yet to be proved!

Ultimately risk assessment must involve two approaches in any study. The first should involve a comparison of costs and benefits within the process itself and with similar processes. The second should determine the risks involved from the very start of the process and involve consideration of factors operating from the point of the extraction of raw materials from the environment to the end use of the products made. It is no longer good practice to consider only what has been produced at the "end of pipe" but to review the process as a whole.

RISK MANAGEMENT

We cannot avoid risks because it is neither practicable nor desirable since we have always accepted risk in order to make progress. The idea is to control and live with risks via the process of risk management.

Risk assessment is largely a scientific process whilst risk management is a decision making process which uses risk assessment. Risk management involves a wide range of expertise on the part of the practitioner, involving political, economic and social considerations.

There are in essence four ways of enabling the management of risk. Having identified the hazard and associated risks, one can **reduce the risk**. This can be done, for example, by designing more efficient incinerators and placing them in less well-populated areas or by finding a less harmful substance as a substitute for the hazard material. In case of an accident there should be in place a system for **damage limitation**. This might take the form of ensuring that proper crisis planning has taken place within a process to minimise risk and prepare for accidents. A third way involves **accepting and sharing of risk**. Here, a waste site which is in someone's backyard is not endangering everyone equally. Therefore part of the management process might entail the compensation of people who are at greater risk in case of any injury. Legislation in the form of insurance/taxation processes and higher prices of commodities may need to be managed to reflect what has been done by industry to pay for safety. Finally, **redressment for damage** will play its part and relates to the financial measures taken after an accident has occurred - an interesting point for the victims of asbestos and dioxins.

How can a manufacturer's financial and economic interests be reconciled with the public's perceptions of what constitutes a hazard and a risk? The power and influence of public opinion are great, and if such power is to be harnessed in ways that will benefit the environment in general then proper risk evaluations must be a part of every industrial and commercial process. Such risk assessment must (i) enable everyone to understand what constitutes a hazard and a risk; (ii) remove unnecessary secrecy; (iii) allow access to relevant information and its interpretations. It is unacceptable to receive information from parties with vested interests no matter how honestly presented. They must come from authoritative and independent bodies in which the public has confidence. If this is not available then interpretations by the media or pressure groups may well become accepted by the public, with the possible consequence that objective and rational discussion may be obscured by the language of emotion.

FACT FILE 2.1
Dioxins - the materials

Dioxins are a group of *organic chemicals*, which contain *benzene* rings and the elements carbon, hydrogen, oxygen and chlorine. They are specifically polychlorinated dibenzo-p-dioxins and polychlorinated dibenzofurans. These chemical names are cumbersome and so are often abbreviated to PCDDs and PCDFs respectively. The chemical that has caused most concern is 2,3,7,8-tetrachlorodibenzo-p-dioxin or TCDD for short.

These chemicals are not easily broken down physically or biologically. Usually, the more chlorine atoms they have in their molecular structures the more stable they are and thus the more difficult to get rid of. They are only very slightly soluble in water, but are readily soluble in organic solvents, fats and oils. They chemically bind *(adsorb)* to the surface of soil particles and are not readily released *(desorbed)*. They tend to concentrate in the bottom sediments of water bodies and accumulate in the fatty tissues of fish and other animals.

PCDDs are often the unwanted and accidental by-products in the manufacture of certain herbicides, wood preservatives and other chemical products. The two herbicides used in Agent Orange were derived from 2,4,5- trichlorophenol (TCP). These herbicides were 2,4-dichlorophenoxy acetic acid (2,4-D) and 2,4,5-trichlorophenoxy acetic acid (2,4,5-T). The other chemical present was TCDD.

Dioxins can also be produced by the burning of *chlorine*-containing materials in old, inefficient incinerators. This is due to the presence of insufficient oxygen, low temperatures, and too short a residence time in the furnace area. Modern state-of-the art incinerators do not produce dioxins in quantities likely to cause concern. Other sources of dioxins come from vehicle emissions, domestic and industrial coal combustion, and coal-fired power stations. For many years it was thought that only man-made chemicals and activities produced these compounds. It is now known that natural forest fires and volcanic eruptions also produce a natural background concentration of these materials. Indeed, a bonfire or any wood burning fire will produce dioxins albeit in very small quantities.

Some typical values for the concentration of total PCDD/Fs in the UK are as follows :-

- urban air   3.4 pg/m^3 urban soil   1436 ng/kg
- rural grass   45 ng/kg   human adipose tissue   1.5 µg/kg of fat.

Some typical values of estimated total PCDD/F emissions from known UK sources:-

- municipal waste incinerators   10.9 kg per year
- domestic coal combustion   5.1 kg per year
- industrial coal combustion   7.7 kg per year
- leaded petrol   0.7 kg per year.

FACT FILE 2.2
Asbestos - the material

Asbestos is the generic name given to certain *inorganic* mineral *silicates* that occur in fibrous form. These occur naturally in seams or veins generally between 1 and 20 mm thick, in many *igneous* and *metamorphic* rocks. These minerals belong to one of two large groups of rock-forming materials, the serpentines and the amphiboles. Such fibre can be processed into a variety of materials that are uniquely resistant to fire, heat, and corrosion. chrysotile (white asbestos), the fibrous form of serpentine, is the most important source and constitutes 95% of world production. The largest producer of asbestos is Russia (46% of world production), but the main sources imported to the UK are from Canada and Southern Africa. The main two fibrous forms of the amphiboles, crocidolite (blue asbestos) and amosite (brown asbestos), are now of lesser importance as asbestos sources.

Asbestos rock is usually excavated from open-pit mines and then crushed to free the fibre. These fibres can be spun and woven into fire-resistant textiles, matted into insulating materials, or used with other substances to make more than 2,500 products, including brake linings and clutch pads, roofing and flooring materials, cement, and insulation for electrical circuits. For many of these products, asbestos is almost irreplaceable. No other substance provides stability, strength, and heat resistance so cheaply and efficiently. Nevertheless, manufacturers are now developing materials that can be substituted for asbestos.

FACT FILE 2.3
Diseases caused by asbestos

Asbestos causes several diseases, but the two that are causing considerable concern are asbestosis and mesothelioma. Asbestos is the only known cause of mesothelioma which is a malignant cancer of the pleura (the membrane that surrounds the lungs) or peritoneum (the membrane that lines the abdominal cavity and covers the abdominal organs) for which there is no treatment or cure. Although it can take between 10 to 50 years to develop it is always fatal. Deaths normally occur above the age of 45 for asbestos workers themselves. If death occurs due to these diseases below the age of 45 then it is probably due to indirect exposure. In the pleura, mesothelioma causes pain and breathlessness; tumours in the peritoneum cause enlargement of the abdomen and obstruction of the intestines. Victims of this disease often show minimal fibrosis and no lung cancer. If the exposure has been to a high concentration of asbestos the diseases of the lung are prominent. If exposure has been to a low concentration, then translocation to the pleura becomes more common and hence mesothelioma tends to ensue. Hence the more rigorously controlled asbestos has been, the more likely is the victim to die of the latter disease.

Asbestosis is caused by the replacement of the specialised tissues of the lungs and the pleura by scar tissue. It is similar to the coal-miners' disease pneumoconiosis caused by coal dust, and to silicosis caused by dust containing *silica* which is associated with quartz mining, stone cutting, blasting and tunnelling. Asbestosis tends to progress even when the victim is no longer exposed to asbestos. The disease causes breathlessness and a dry cough, eventually leading to severe disability and death. The period from first exposure to the development of the disease is seldom less than ten years and is usually much longer. Asbestosis increases the risk of developing lung cancer in smokers and non-smokers alike, but the combination of smoking and asbestosis leads to an even greater risk. Asbestosis is a "prescribed" disease which entitles sufferers in the UK to industrial injury benefit.

How does asbestos cause such problems?

The cells lining the *bronchi*, and the larger *bronchioles* of the human respiratory system have whip-like *cilia* at their free surfaces. These normally move dust particles upward towards the *trachea* where they are coughed out. If the size of the dust particle falls below a certain size (4μm or less) then they behave like gas particles. This means that such particles can enter the respiratory bronchioles and then the terminal air sacs *(alveoli)*. Here there are no cilia and therefore the dust particles cannot be removed. In the case of fibrous particles, their ability to move through the air vessels and to reach the alveoli depends mainly on their thickness, e.g. a long but thin fibre is more likely to reach the alveoli than a long fat one. Once in the alveoli *macrophage* cells engulf the asbestos particles. They pass through the alveoli walls and the walls of the larger bronchioles, blood vessel walls and through the pleura. If it moves through a blood vessel wall and into the blood then the dust particle may be carried to another organ. It may, for example, move into the pleura where it can be transferred somewhere else and cause damage. Because of the process just described asbestos workers tend to suffer from gastrointestinal, biliary and renal cancers.

Further Reading Chapter 2

Agent Orange Risks Assessed, Science, 1993, **261**, No.5122

B.J.Alloway & D.C.Ayres, *Chemical Principles of Environmental Pollution*, Blackie Academic, London, 1993

R.Bate (Ed.), *What Risk?*, Oxford, Butterworth-Heinemann, 1997

P.Calow, *Controlling Environmental Risks from Chemicals*, Chichester, John Wiley, 1997

P.Calow (Ed), *Handbook of Environmental Risk Assessment & Management*, Oxford, Blackwell Science, 1998

H.Carmichael, *Risk; A Human Science*, Chemistry in Britain, 1998, **34**, No.4

G.C.A. Dickson, *Risk Analysis*, 2nd Ed., London, Witherby & the Institute of Risk Management, 1991

R. Doll, *Effects on Health of Exposure to Asbestos*, London, Health & Safety Commission, HMSO, 1985

Dioxin's Other Face, Science News, 1992, **141**, No.2

B.Ellis & J.F.Rees, *Contaminated Land Remediation in the UK with Reference to Risk Assessment: Two Case Studies, Water & Environmental Management:* Journal of the Institute of Water & Environmental Management, 1995, **9**, No.1

R.Fairman & N.Parkinson, *Risk Assessment*, Environmental Health, June 1992

R.E.Hester & R.M.Harrison (Ed.), *Risk Assessment & Risk Management*, Cambridge, Royal Society of Chemistry, 1998

E.R.A. Merewether, *Report on Effects of Asbestos Dust on the Lungs and dust Suppression in the Asbestos Industry*, London, His Majesty's Stationery Office, 1930

Mineral Wools: Do They Cause Cancer?, The Safety & Health Practioner, April 1995

Science: The Return of Agent Orange, Time, 1993, **142**, No.6

J.Turton, *Killer Dust,* The Guardian Weekend, May 8, 1993

A.H. Westing & E.W.Pfeiffer, *Dioxins in Vietnam*, Science, 1995, **270**, No.5234

CHAPTER 3

SUSTAINABLE RESOURCE MANAGEMENT
the life cycle of a steel cooking pan,
cradle to grave

An explanation of the term "life-cycle assessment" is given with particular reference to a steel cooking pan and the production of the iron it contains. The discussion includes the importance of minimising the use of natural material and energy resources, and waste production. The general principles of environmental management are outlined, followed by a discussion of the ways in which environmental management can be carried out.

THE LIFE CYCLE OF A STEEL COOKING PAN

When you are using an ordinary steel cooking pan to prepare a Sunday lunch, the last thing you will probably be thinking of is where the steel came from, what was involved in the pan's manufacture, how it came to be in the shop from which it was bought, or what will happen to it when it comes to the end of its useful life. Most people would not think in terms of an inanimate object like a cooking pan as having a "life-cycle" which can be compared in some ways to that of a living thing.

In the manufacture of the steel cooking pan, as in any product or process, there are movements of material and energy both into and out of that process throughout its life-cycle. If we can control and reduce the amounts of materials and energy involved then the Earth's physical resources will last longer, more time will be available to search for possible substitute materials and ways of recycling, and there will be less polluting wastes finding their way into our environment. The first step then might be to review the life-cycle of a product in order to identify where materials and energy are involved.

A cooking pan starts its life (cf. Figure 3.1) when the raw materials are extracted from the Earth's crust by the mining of iron *ore*, *coal* and *limestone*. This is followed by the removal of soil, rock and other impurities to concentrate the iron ore before it can be converted into the metal *iron*. A similar physical separation might also be necessary in the cases of the coal and limestone. Before the coal is used it has to be converted into *coke* by heating it in the absence of air. This is done on site in a modern steel plant. The chemical extraction of the iron metal occurs in a blast furnace where the ore, mixed with coke and limestone, is subjected to a blast of very hot air. It is usually necessary to transport the iron ore, coal and limestone to the blast furnace site. The iron produced from the blast furnace contains a small percentage of impurities, mainly carbon, which causes it to be far too brittle and hard to be used to produce items like a cooking utensil. Steel is produced by blowing oxygen gas onto the molten iron, so converting these impurities to gaseous oxides that are removed from the furnace. A cooking pan must be resistant to staining and corrosion by hot liquids and is therefore made of stainless steel, and so the elements *chromium* and *nickel* must be added. This type of steel is made in an electric arc furnace where ordinary molten steel is mixed with the appropriate amounts of these elements in the absence of oxygen. When the steel is of the correct composition it is run out of the furnace and allowed to cool in the form of sheets.

The steel is delivered to the manufacturers of kitchen utensils who will press out the shape of the pan from the sheet steel, attach a handle and produce cooking pans in their thousands every week. The finished pans are distributed to the wholesale and retail industries who sell them to you, the consumer. One day you will decide the pan has ceased to perform its function properly and consign it to the dustbin, where it will become part of the domestic waste stream. Throughout this "cradle to the grave" life-cycle of the pan, several material resources together with vast amounts of various

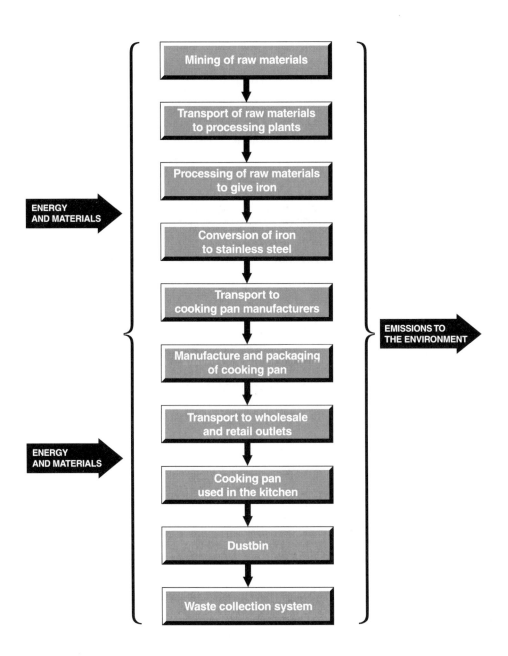

Figure 3.1 Life Cycle of a Steel Cooking Pan

forms of energy have been used. Various types of wastes are produced which have to be disposed of and treated. There are thus many points of interaction with the environment throughout the production of the pan. Figure 3.2 shows a very simplified diagram of the energy and material flows in the blast furnace part of the production.

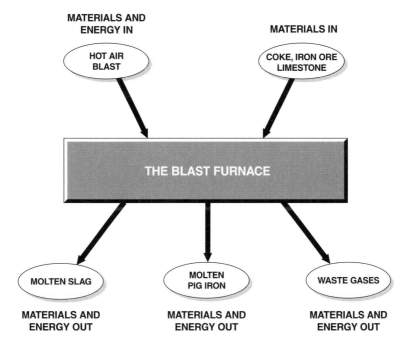

Figure 3.2 The Blast Furnace - Movement of Materials & Energy

How can manufacturers minimise these interactions? How can the use of resources be maximised so that the use of more expensive alternatives is delayed? How can resources be conserved? The answers to these questions lie in the concept of "sustainable resource management" which involves as its central idea the control of all forms of waste and the prolonging of the availability of existing resources.

ENVIRONMENTAL CONSERVATION AND CONCERNS

In order to understand why sustainable resource management is so important it is perhaps necessary to examine what is meant by environmental conservation since the two are intimately related. One definition of conservation is "the careful use of natural resources such as air, water, soil, plants, animals, rocks and minerals". Conservation also includes the maintenance of such amenities as national parks, wildlife centres, sites of particular historic interest, wilderness areas, etc. The natural resources of a country are often directly related to its economy and the standard of living of its people. Thus the wasteful use or even non-use of those resources could result in both short and long term social and economic damage.

Natural resources are of two main types, renewable and non-renewable. The former include all animal and plant life, whilst the latter are composed of fossil fuels, ores and minerals. Non-renewable resources are the ones giving rise to serious concerns. It has been clear for years that many non-renewable resources are being used up at a faster rate than fresh usable sources are being discovered or substitutes found. The sustainability of resource usage requires that natural resources are managed efficiently and whenever possible conserved. Such is the worry about our resources that waste production and its dumping into the environment is now viewed by many as an almost criminal squandering of our Earth's resources.

Growing fears over the future availability of natural resources have led to calls for reductions in the amount of waste produced in any process, and for an increase in the ways in which materials and/or energy can be recovered from waste. Such recovery would slow down the exhaustion of non-renewable resources and might even lower the use of such resources to the rate of their replenishment.

Pollutants, which are by-products of resource use, have given rise to much public concern. In the past, the air, land and the oceans have been used as sinks, and a means of diluting and dispersing all kinds of waste products. When the waste has been at low concentrations then the environment has been able to buffer its effects with little or no changes occurring in environmental conditions. As the human population and its activities have increased then more and more waste has been released into the environment. The natural buffering ability of the environment has not been sufficient in being able to cope with increased levels of waste "dumping". The consequences have been a change in environmental conditions and, in some cases, major disturbances in environmental quality. When dealing with environmental matters consideration must be given to a variety of factors which include the extraction of the maximum value from a resource together with the minimisation of waste production and hence pollution. We must look beyond, though not exclude, risk and safety considerations and examine ways in which efficient resource management can be achieved which provides a much longer-term use of known resources.

When a non-renewable resource is used, where does the material go and do we in fact lose it forever? In other words, is the material destroyed? In order to answer these questions we will look more closely at one aspect of steel production, namely the way in which iron is produced in the blast furnace.

The Production of Iron in the Blast Furnace

Iron ore was formed millions of years ago and is an example of a natural, non-renewable resource. There are several different types of iron ores but the main one that is used is hematite which contains an oxide of iron, i.e. a chemical combination of the elements oxygen and iron. The purpose of the blast furnace is to enable the separation of the oxygen from the iron.

You will remember that the materials put into the blast furnace are iron ore, coke and limestone. Blasts of very hot air are then blown through small holes in the bottom of the furnace. The coke burns by reaction with oxygen in the hot air to produce gaseous *carbon monoxide* and a large quantity of heat. The carbon monoxide then combines with the oxygen from the iron oxide to form iron and *carbon dioxide* plus a smaller quantity of heat. Molten iron runs to the bottom of the furnace where it is tapped off periodically. (See Fact File 3.1 for more details.)

One of the fundamental laws of chemistry is the one known as the Law of Conservation of Mass. This states that in any chemical reaction the total mass of the materials that are present at the start of the reaction is the same as the total mass of the materials produced when the reaction is over. Hence in the case of the reaction between the coke and oxygen (the reactants) to give carbon monoxide gas (the product), the total mass of the reactants and the total mass of the product will be the same. Similarly, for the reaction between iron oxide and carbon monoxide to produce iron and carbon dioxide, i.e.

carbon + oxygen = carbon monoxide

iron oxide + carbon monoxide = iron + carbon dioxide

Thus when we describe the iron ore as a non-renewable resource we don't mean the atoms from which it is made are destroyed but, during the production of iron, its atoms are separated and rearranged with the consequent liberation of heat energy. Hence, the products contain less energy than the reactants. Matter has not been destroyed but has been reorganised, in this case, in a more useful way.

However, once the iron ore and the coal used to make coke are removed from the environment they are no longer available to produce iron. Indeed, the coke ultimately becomes carbon dioxide which eventually finds its way into the atmosphere. Iron ore and coal occur in large quantities in various parts of the world. However, there is not a bottomless pit of these resources. When we use them to produce iron we effectively "destroy" in hours what it took many millions of years to form.

Fortunately, iron-based metals are recycled and reused on a very large scale - a good example of resource management.

SOME GENERAL PRINCIPLES OF ENVIRONMENTAL MANAGEMENT

Most people, rightly or wrongly, identify industry and manufacturing processes as the major culprits responsible for the pollution of our environment and the wasteful users of resources. Industry is responding to those charges by examining ways in which they can not only make a profit but also link that profit with the more efficient use of resources and the demands of their consumers and society in general, whist still using their existing infrastructure. Efficient resource use by manufacturers depends upon the application of self-imposed, specially designed, coherent environmental management systems. Several general managerial principles can be identified which can be used as a guide to the development of such systems.

Firstly, it must be recognised that a variety of information and management tools are required to enable the control of the interactions of a business with the environment. For example, some of these tools are applied in a quite specific manner and include scientific investigative techniques and compliance with regulations. Others are of a less obvious environmental nature and are based on more traditional business approaches such as determining what consumers require and how they behave.

Secondly, any decision-making in environmental management will involve the careful integration of the results obtained by these different tools. Although numbers and facts will be available to aid decision taking, both objective and subjective judgements will need to be made by managers based on their previous experiences. There will be times when a "balancing act" will need to be done, i.e. determining whether a negative aspect of a production process is outweighed by a positive one. Often managers will need to make decisions that are affected by the lack or poor quality of information.

The third guiding principle involves the need for careful planning. This should develop cost effective plans to reduce waste from processes, packages and products; minimise waste, energy use and emissions to the environment; statistically analyse data, quantify and evaluate results; be recognised by the company as being effective and efficient, and thus worthy of owning; finally is capable of being used elsewhere in the companies operations.

The fourth principle involves the acquisition and use of easily checkable and understandable data in terms of its objectivity/subjectivity, validity, origin and quality.

The fifth area is the need for a manufacturer to balance any advantages in sharing environmental information with society at large against the necessity of that company not to give away information which will adversely effect its competitiveness.

Finally, environmental improvements cannot be judged in terms of "burden" or "impact" alone. Real improvements to products and services can only be evaluated based on the balance between their value to society and the environmental burdens. A product which significantly reduces environmental burdens can only deliver its environmental benefit if it is sold in place of an environmentally less desirable alternative. Only products that offer good performance and value (so are sold and used), and that simultaneously have a reduced environmental burden, will deliver any environmental benefit.

Clearly, industrial companies have much to consider before they can respond to specific environmental demands made by society - effective and sustained changes based on the above general principles cannot be made overnight.

HOW CAN ENVIRONMENTAL MANAGEMENT BE CARRIED OUT?

The overall goal of environmental management is ecological and economic sustainability. This can be made possible by using an environmental management framework consisting of four basic elements which underpin the general principles described in the last section, i.e.

- ensuring of human and environmental safety;
- obeying regulations and laws;
- efficient resource use and waste management, and
- addressing the concerns of society.

The first two elements are prerequisites for doing business whilst the last two, though not compulsory, are emerging business needs. Manufacturers are directly responsible for managing the environmental effects of the production stages within their own factory gates as well as those arising from the use of their products. Manufacturers also exert a certain level of influence on other external phases in the life-cycle of a product, ranging from resource extraction and the production of materials to the proper disposal of waste.

Any human activity, whether it is in the manufacturing industries, service industries or society in general, must take into account the safety of humans and the environment. In the case of the cooking pan, safety must be ensured during all stages of its manufacture, use and disposal. As indicated in Chapter 2, there are well-established tools for both human health and ecological risk assessment to enable safety to be ensured. Human health risk assessments are performed to protect both workers at manufacturing sites and the consumer in the home. Ecological risk assessments are done to evaluate the safety of both discharges from manufacturing plants and those from the consumer's home. Both types of assessment require a comparison of exposure effects, i.e. the level of a substance that comes into contact with a human or the environment compared with the level that could cause harm. Throughout the steel pan production chemicals are involved which could cause human and environmental problems. If they are released into the environment, each individual chemical can cause its own problems. Indeed, some less harmful chemicals can be changed by environmental processes (e.g. biodegradation) into new and more harmful ones. To determine the level of harm a chemical can cause in the environment means that a wide variety of animal and plant life must be considered. If it is predicted that exposure may cause an adverse effect then the risk should be deemed unacceptable and should be reduced by limiting or substituting the use of the chemical. To ensure an adequate safety margin, the predicted exposure must be reliably known and significantly lower than effect levels. Product safety is the first environmental management responsibility of any manufacturer. It must be systematically incorporated into all stages of the manufacture, use and disposal of a product.

The activities of companies in modern industrial societies are monitored and regulated by external authorities (local government, health and safety officials, etc.). It is the responsibility of a management system to ensure compliance with the specific local and national regulations. Typically, a company can check each of its manufacturing sites to determine if emissions and wastes are complying with the locally legislated or permitted levels. Some national governments require much more than this. For example, in the USA legislation requires manufacturers to test and report on the presence/absence of over 300 specially listed chemicals. Holland requires data to be kept and reported by companies on the annual consumption of different packaging materials as well as progress in achieving reductions. The use of all chemical substances in the UK is also the subject of regulatory compliance. All chemicals have to be assessed for safety purposes before use. Such assessment requires the chemical and physical properties, toxicology and ecotoxicology data to be listed and an appropriate safety procedure dossier to be compiled. Chemicals in the UK are required to be classified in terms of dangerous properties and packed and labelled accordingly.

Saving materials and energy saves a company money. This also reduces interactions with the environment and thus pleases the public. The efficient use of resources and the management of wastes have always made good economic and social sense. Today, they are also required for sustainable development and have therefore become part of environmental management. The continual monitoring of the use of resources and waste management together with the identification of ways to increase efficiencies requires consideration of the whole life-cycle of a product or service and all that may effect the environment. It must be ensured, though, that any improvements in one part of the life-cycle or in one aspect of the environment do not cause a greater problem elsewhere. Whilst it is normally preferable to design the problems out of a system at the design and development stages rather than using "end-of-pipe" solutions, a complete review of the system is necessary to determine the most appropriate environmental and economic route to take.

There are several methods that can be used to ensure a total quality, life-cycle approach. All of these methods work by following and accounting for material and energy flows into and out of a process. The first is based on the monitoring of the waste produced and energy consumed at a manufacturing site. Here the emissions to air, land and water at the site from the various manufacturing processes and products are monitored and reported. The information obtained can make it possible to "design out" or otherwise re-use wastes. The second method concerns the monitoring of material consumption and determining ways of reducing it at a product site. The third, and the one strongly advocated in this book, is based on the **Life-Cycle Inventory (LCI)** approach. This attempts to calculate the total material and energy flows on a complete product system basis and its emissions to the environment, from cradle to grave (see Chapter 5 for further details). It maps out, on a large scale, all environmental burdens associated with providing a particular product to society. This allows an analysis of the whole product life-cycle, and is especially useful in ensuring that problems are not merely shifted from one life-cycle area to another. Another particular use for this tool is in identifying which changes in a product's life-cycle produce the most significant environmental improvements.

The information provided by the above three tools is used in yet another tool called **"eco-design"**. The objective here is to find ways (i.e. reuse or recycling) to use the wastes produced at various points in a manufacturing process and so minimise the use of "end-of-pipe" solutions.

Internal auditing of a manufacturing site should be carried out in order to check that the method(s) used to ensure efficient resource use and waste management are doing their job correctly. Auditing can also be a useful procedure when carried out with co-operation between manufacturers and suppliers. Although done less formally than an internal audit, this can lead to an overall improvement in the environmental profile of a product. An integration of the manufacturer, who understands the end product, together with the supplier who knows the raw materials, often leads to developments with a better overall environmental performance.

It is clear that the efficient use of resources and waste management will help to minimise costs and so reflect positively on a company's financial status and profit margins. Thus both the company and the environment will benefit.

In addressing the concerns of society, a company needs to understand the people to whom it sells and the society in which it operates. This requires an appreciation of and a response to the prevailing political climate (government) together with the identification of consumer needs (appropriateness of the product) as well as society's concerns (public opinion and fears). The tools that are used to do this fall into two broad areas:

- observation, identification and understanding of society's needs;
- responding to the concerns in an appropriate manner.

One method of finding out about public concerns is the use of opinion surveys. However, it must be remembered that it is important to understand the opinion of the "silent majority" as well as the vocal activist. The additional tool of liaison with key opinion leaders, scientists and government officials can also be of use, since these groups often help to frame and develop public debate. Responses to society's concerns involves:

- the development and organisation of appropriate data to improve understanding of issues;

- information sharing through public presentations and publications (including advertising);
- active participation and co-operation in groups working in the public, scientific and industrial sectors to find reasonable solutions. Companies and their industries will also engage in lobbying within the political process.

Effective response requires trust between the company and other social partners. Given the suspicion of industry by the general public, individual companies must respond by being more open and informative about what they do and why they do it. There is, for example, a growing practice for companies to publish an annual report on their environmental management processes and results.

ENVIRONMENTAL DECISION MAKING

Throughout the process of environmental management, decisions have to be made at various levels. Decisions are far easier to take where safety and other legislative requirements are laid down. Other decisions are much less clear cut and depend upon a variety of information produced by many environmental and economic tools. Such decision taking, it can be argued, would be aided by adopting a life-cycle inventory approach. Whatever the outcomes, the final decision will be an amalgam of environmental and economic influences, since an environmentally-improved product will only deliver environmental benefit if it sells in place of a less environmentally desirable option. In this sense it is you, the consumer, who may dictate whether or not a product will have an influence on the environment.

A range of methods and tools that can help a company to reduce waste, conserve resources and therefore reduce environmental impact has been described above. No one method or tool is the answer to all problems; they are mutually supporting and overlap in some of their objectives. The most important basis for any sound decision taking remains the quality of the input data used and how it is analysed and interpreted. The latter is certainly based upon experience and will depend on the application by managers of well balanced judgement and sound knowledge.

Environmental management is clearly a responsibility that must be shared between the company and its partners (suppliers, customers, consumers, the government). Traditionally there have been relatively simple requirements for a company to satisfy, e.g. comply with the law, satisfy customers and shareholders, and ensure compatibility with public utilities such as sewage works. Recognising the need for collaboration to achieve environmental improvements involves another dimension and brings other relationships to the fore, such as those between customers and suppliers, waste managers, concerned interest groups and others. The whole process of environmental management is very complex and perhaps raises the question "Who would want to be an environmental manager?"

FACT FILE 3.1

Coal is a solid fossil fuel of plant origin. Some 345-280 million years ago (Carboniferous Period) much of the earth was covered by a vigorous growth of vegetation and swamps. Many of these plants were types of ferns, some being as large as trees. When this vegetation died and collapsed into water it gradually decomposed. As this decomposition took place, the vegetable matter lost hydrogen and oxygen atoms leaving a deposit with a high percentage by mass of carbon. These deposits formed peat bogs. As time passed, layers of sediments were deposited on top of peat which was covered with water. The pressure of these overlying layers, together with movements of the Earth's crust and volcanic heat, caused compression and hardening of these deposits, thus producing coal.

Coke is formed when coal is heated in ovens to about 1500C in a much reduced supply of air. Other products that are formed are coal gas, ammoniacal liquor and coal tar. Typically one metric tonne of coal will produce 670-720 kg of coke containing about 92% by mass of carbon. Coke can be used as a high energy containing fuel, and as a source of organic chemicals when combined with oxygen and hydrogen. It is used on a very large scale as an industrial reducing agent in the blast furnace for the production of both iron and zinc.

The Blast Furnace. The blast furnace is charged with iron ore, coke and limestone in weighed proportions according to the iron ore used. The chemical reactions that go on inside the furnace are very complex but the principal ones are as follows.

Near the base of the furnace, coke burns in the very hot blast of air to produce carbon monoxide,

$$2C(s) + O_2 = 2CO(g)$$

This reaction is strongly exothermic, i.e. gives out a lot of heat, which raises the temperature inside to above 1500C. Near the top of the furnace the carbon monoxide gas reacts with the solid iron ore to produce a spongy form of iron,

$$Fe_2O_3 (s) + 3CO(g) = 2Fe(s) + 3CO_2(g)$$

The iron melts as its sinks through the hotter parts of the furnace and collects at the bottom of the furnace. Here it is tapped off and allowed to cool. The solid iron at this stage is called Pig-iron or Cast iron.

The function of the limestone is to help remove earthy materials which contain, for example, sand (SiO_2) that can silt up the furnace, react with the iron and generally cause problems.

The limestone is decomposed by the heat to give calcium oxide (quick lime),

$$CaCO_3 (s) = CaO(s) + CO_2(g)$$

This calcium oxide reacts with the earthy materials to give a molten slag of silicates,

$$CaO(s) + SiO_2(s) = CaSiO_3(l)$$

The slag collects on top of the molten iron and can again be tapped off.

Iron ores occur mainly in the form of oxides of iron. **Hematite** is one of the most important and is represented by the formula Fe_2O_3. It contains 70% of iron by mass. It is blood red in colour and occurs in several forms. Kidney iron-ore is so called because it occurs in red, rounded masses that are not obviously crystalline but resemble kidneys. Specular iron-ore takes a high polish and can be found in beautiful well-shaped crystals. Hematite deposits in workable quantities are found throughout the world. **Limonite** is also known as brown iron or bog iron. This ore is a mixture of hydrated iron oxides and can be represented by FeO.OH. It has a lustrous brown, yellow or black appearance, is often streaky, porous and mixed with sand and clay. **Magnetite** is the most magnetic of minerals in that it is attracted to a magnet. It is a brittle mixed oxide of iron, Fe_2O_3 .FeO, which appears black and shiny. Magnetite which is itself magnetic and will attract iron is called lodestone. There are other ores of iron but these tend to be of lesser importance than the oxides.

FACT FILE 3.2

To illustrate the complexity of dealing with a life-cycle approach to environmental management we need only to mention some of the factors involved in the production and supply of one of the raw materials, i.e. coal, to a UK steel works. Initial considerations show that coal is dirty to handle, costly to transport, has a lower energy content when compared mass for mass with other fuels, and is far more polluting.

In 1990 in the UK coal when used as a fuel was responsible for 75% of sulphur dioxide emissions, 29% of NO_x emissions, 40% of carbon dioxide emissions and 37% of black smoke. All of these give rise to smog, acid rain and "greenhouse gas" problems. Certainly all of these pollutants are produced in the manufacture of steel. Coal mines in the UK also produced 19% of total methane gas emissions, which was equivalent to some 850 000 tonnes per year. Although there has been a decline in the number of operating deep mines, in 1990-91, 45 million tonnes of spoil were produced by coal mining. This contributed to spoil tips that are unsightly and can contaminate water resources with acid run-off. In addition to this, coal-mining produces some 5 million tonnes of minestone spoil per year. This was disposed of on beaches and by dumping at sea. By 1995 British Coal were required to find alternative sites to beaches, and by 1997 an alternative to dumping at sea.

Coal mining has created and continues to create derelict land, though attempts are now being made to reclaim some of it. Yet another environmental problem is subsidence caused by underground mines. There has been an increase in the number of applications in the UK to develop surface open cast mines. Local public opposition to these has been intense, providing a testing time for managers at all levels in the coal industry.

Further Reading Chapter 3

G.Jones & G Hollier, *Resources, Society & Environmental Management,* London. Paul Chapman, 1997

A.S. Mather & K.Chapman, *Environmental Resources*, Essex, Longman,1995

S.Moor, Doomsday Delayed: America's Surprisingly Bright Natural Resource Future, *IPI Policy Report no.118*, Lewisville, Texas, The Institute for Policy Innovation, 1992

T.O'Riordan (Ed), *Environmental Science for Environmental Management*, Essex, Longman Scientific & Technical, 1995

L.Owen & T.Unwin, *Environmental Management, Readings and Case Studies*, Oxford, Blackwell Publishers, 1997

L.G.Smith, *Impact Assessment & Sustainable Resource Management*, Harlow, Longman Scientific & Technical, 1993

CHAPTER 4

SOLID WASTES
what are they and how can they be managed?

The various ways in which waste substances can be classified are described. Solid waste in particular is examined and its various components identified. Environmental concerns over the production and disposal of solid waste production are examined. Past and current techniques of handling waste are described, and the benefits and limitations of each presented. Examples of some of the environmental effects of non-existent and poor waste disposal methods are given throughout.

At first glance, an old newspaper; potato peelings; the exhaust fumes from a leaded-petrol car engine, and the spray from a *CFCs*-based aerosol can would seem to have little in common. However, a closer examination shows they all involve waste in one form or another.

In the cases of the newspaper and the potato peelings most people would probably put them in a dustbin as unwanted rubbish. Alternatively, the newspaper might be taken to a recycling bin and the potato peelings placed on a compost heap. When leaded petrol is burned in the internal combustion engine of the motor car, it produces fumes which enter our atmosphere. Most of these products are hazardous and enter the atmosphere as *pollutants*. For example, one component of motorcar exhaust fumes has been blamed for affecting the mental health of young children whilst others are thought to cause lung related diseases. The nature of these pollutants and how widely spread they have become makes it extremely difficult technically to remove them from our environment. *CFCs* have been used as the coolant in refrigerators and air conditioning equipment, as well as cleaning solvents and the propellant in aerosol sprays. These man-made chemicals have been allowed to enter the atmosphere via evaporation, uncontrolled spraying and leakage from scrapped refrigerators. *CFCs* are suspected of helping to destroy the *ozone layer* which is our principal shield against the sun's harmful ultra-violet radiation. It is suspected that the decrease in ozone has led in the case of human beings to an increase in skin cancers, eye cataracts and a reduction in the ability to resist infections. In addition, ozone depletion has apparently interfered with *photosynthesis* processes and the growth of oceanic *plankton*. The removal of *CFCs* from manufacturing processes and worn out, broken equipment, has been easy. Their removal from our atmosphere will probably be impossible.

WHAT IS WASTE?

To you the word "waste" probably conjures up visions of litter or the dustbin and the rubbish it contains. In the cases of the newspaper and potato peelings we are obviously dealing with domestic waste. But what about the other examples quoted above? What does the word "waste" mean in the context of our environment?

Waste material is produced as a result of human or animal activities. Various words such as rubbish, trash, garbage, and so on are often used as a substitute for the word "waste". Whatever it is called, waste is unwanted by whoever or whatever produces it and is seen to be useless, often hazardous and of no economic or other value. Industrial, commercial and domestic wastes usually contain the same materials which were used to make the useful products from which the waste originated. Perhaps the best way to deal with waste might be to restore some kind of value to it, thus removing it from its classification as waste? The major problem in trying to restore value is that much of the waste that has already been allowed into the environment is a complex mixture of a wide variety of materials, often of unknown composition. A large expenditure of money would thus be necessary to finance the identification of the components of waste and to separate them effectively. As indicated above, in the case of leaded petrol it would be impossible to collect and concentrate any of the waste products in quantities which would be economically viable. Hence the relationship between how mixed up the waste is, how concentrated the components are and what value they have is a very important property of waste and can dictate how it is handled and treated. Waste can be classified in the ways shown in Table 4.1.

Table 4.1   The Classification of Waste.

WASTE CLASSIFICATION	EXAMPLES
By physical state, i.e. gas, solid or liquid	Sauce bottle - a solid CFCs - gases Waste from petrol engines - gases and liquids
How the original material was used	Sauce bottle - packaging waste. Potato peelings - food waste
By type of material	Sauce bottle - glass Newspaper - paper Aluminium can - metal
Chemical properties	Paper - burns easily Potato peelings - compostable
According to health hazard	CFCs - not toxic to humans Lead dibromide - toxic to humans
Where it was used	Potato peelings - domestic waste Sauce bottle - domestic waste CFCs - domestic and industrial waste

In this chapter we are going to examine solid waste and in particular the waste which is probably the most familiar to us, domestic solid waste. The major components of solid waste are given in Table 4.2. From this table it can be seen that domestic waste contains essentially rubbish and ashes. Although domestic waste accounts for only a relatively small part of the total amount of all solid waste produced, it is still produced in vast amounts. Typically, in the UK 20 000 000 tonnes of domestic waste a year is produced which is equivalent to about 348 kilograms per person (cf. Table 4.3 for comparisons with other developed countries). There are several good reasons for investigating domestic waste. Firstly, it is the waste that the general public have the most contact with and thus has great political and social significance. Secondly, household waste is one of the most difficult sources of waste to manage effectively because it is a complex mixture of a wide variety of materials present in relatively small proportions. Its composition depends on a number of factors which can include seasonal variations (winter waste in your dustbin, for example, differs significantly from summer waste), the geographical position of a country, and whether it has been derived from rural or urban communities. In contrast, commercial, industrial and other waste materials tend to be much larger in bulk and more homogeneous in nature. Thus it can be argued that if an effective way can be developed to manage household waste then it should be possible to transfer the skills and resources used to the treatment of other sources of waste.

Table 4.2 The Components of Solid Waste

COMPONENT NAME	ORIGIN OF COMPONENT
RUBBISH	decomposable wastes from food combustible materials, e.g. paper, wood non-combustible materials, e.g. glass, metal
ASHES	residues from combustible solid fuels
MINING & QUARRYING WASTE	residues from mines, e.g. slag heaps, rock piles, coal refuse piles
LARGE SIZED WASTE	construction and demolition debris
SEWAGE TREATMENT SOLIDS	sewage treatment screens, settled solids, biomass sludge
AGRICULTURAL WASTE	farm animal manure, crop remains
INDUSTRIAL WASTE	chemicals, sands, plastics, etc.

Table 4.3 Typical Annual Municipal Solid Waste figures for some Developed Countries (Year 1990)

COUNTRY	ANNUAL MUNICIPAL SOLID WASTE (Tons)	EQUIVALENT PER PERSON (Kilograms)
Australia	10 000 000	680
Belgium	3 410 000	343
Canada	12 600 000	525
Denmark	2 430 000	475
Finland	3 100 000	624
France	20 320 000	328
Germany	27 958 000	350
Italy	20 033 000	348
Japan	50 991 000	410
Netherlands	7 430 000	497
New Zealand	1 528 000	488
Norway	2 000 000	472
Spain	12 546 000	322
Sweden	3 200 000	374
Switzerland	3 000 000	441
UK	20 000 000	348
United States	184 000 000	720

Adapted from: *Integrated Solid Waste Management* by P.R.White, et al

SOLID WASTE DISPOSAL METHODS

For many years the main concerns about solid waste management were centred on health and safety. Whilst this is still true, there is now a much wider awareness of the need to recognise and respond to the effects of both solid waste production and its management on the environment in general. Two new major areas of concern can now be identified: the conservation of resources and pollution of the environment. Many of the techniques used in the disposal of solid wastes have in the past contributed to the destruction of useful resources and to the addition of obnoxious materials to our environment. In Great Britain and many other countries a much more enlightened approach now pervades disposal methods and more careful attention is paid to their effects on our environment.

A variety of methods for the disposal of solid waste have been developed which include recycling, composting, biogasification, heat treatment and landfilling. In most of the developed and emerging nations, the disposal of solid waste in landfill sites or by dumping is by far the most common method. Thermal or heat treatment (burning) accounts for most of the waste not disposed of in these ways. Composting of waste accounts for a quite insignificant amount. Which disposal method is used usually depends upon cost, which itself depends very significantly on local circumstances. In order to illustrate the different ways in which waste can be disposed of, we will examine what could happen to the newspaper you have finished reading and no longer want.

Landfill is probably the cheapest and simplest means of solid waste disposal if done in a sanitary fashion, and is the only method which deals immediately with all of the waste (cf. Figure 4.1). Your newspaper could be placed in such a landfill where, over a long period of time, it would rot. Note that all other methods of waste treatment themselves produce waste, which in turn has to be added to landfill. Landfill sites will always be necessary for the treatment of solid waste. Any suitable land must be situated within reasonable travelling distance of the waste source because the cost of transport would become too expensive. The UK and most other European countries continue to use landfilling as the main waste disposal method. However, environmental pressures and the increasing cost of land in the UK are having an effect on the availability of land for new sites.

Land filling does not always involve the creation of a dedicated hole in the ground! In many countries, solid waste has been used to fill exhausted quarries and clay pits and therefore could be described as contributing to land reclamation, i.e. a form of conservation. In the UK above ground structures such as slag and rubbish heaps which have been built up by past generations have joined the natural contours of the surrounding district via landscaping techniques. Other countries like Japan and China have/are using solid wastes to "sea-fill" thus producing man-made islands in Tokyo Bay and extensions to runway facilities in Hong Kong harbour. In modern landfill methodology, the solid waste is spread in thin layers, each of which is

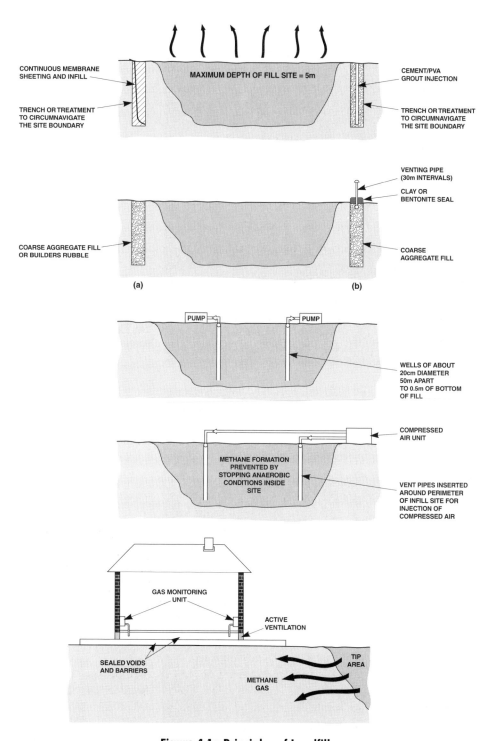

Figure 4.1a Principles of Landfill

Solid waste arrives!

The Catterpillar tractor spreads out the waste prior to its compaction.

A mound of compacted waste is covered with soil.

The size of the place! The site covers approximately 150 acres. Note the "catcher" to the left, which helps prevent paper from being blown away.

Figure 4.1b The Well Managed Harewood Whin Landfill Site, N. Yorks, UK

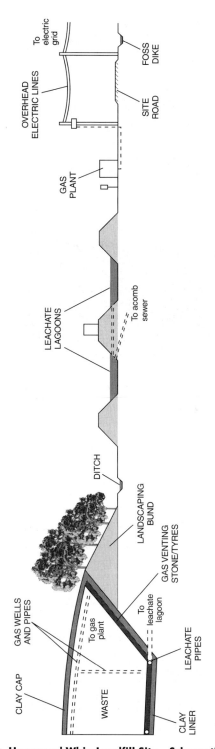

Figure 4.1c Harewood Whin Landfill Site - Schematic Diagram

compacted by the use of heavy vehicles before the next layer is added. When about three metres (ten feet) thickness of waste has been laid down, it is covered by a thin layer of clean soil, which itself is then compacted. Great care has to be taken in the construction and placing of landfill sites so that local pollution does not occur. Pollution of surface and groundwater by *leaching* is minimised by lining the hole and contouring the landfill site, compacting and planting the cover, selecting proper soil, diverting upland drainage, and placing waste in sites not subject to flooding or high groundwater levels. As described in Chapter 1, gases can be generated in landfills via *anaerobic* decomposition of the organic solid waste (including your newspaper) which can result in explosions unless proper ventilation is installed. Very expensive methods of controlling landfill gas have been based either on the prevention of gas emissions or on the prevention of the gas from entering into critical or confined spaces. Figure 4.1 shows how the lateral migration of gas can be controlled. In some parts of the world, landfill sites are operated as large "bioreactors" in which the water content of the landfill is carefully controlled to maximise the production of methane gas. The methane gas is then used in heating applications or for power generation, and thus can contribute to recovery of the costs involved in land acquisition, site construction, site operation, site closure and its long term monitoring and aftercare.

Your newspaper could undergo **Thermal (heat) Treatment** (cf. Figure 4.2) which can consist of three different processes. The most well known is the mass burning, or incineration, of domestic waste in large incinerator plants. As normal domestic waste your newspaper could be burned at your local municipal incinerator to produce an ash and energy. It is also possible that the newspaper may be included in two "select burn" processes where combustible fractions from solid waste are burned as fuels. These fuels, which include paper waste of all kinds, can be separated from the mixed domestic waste mechanically to form what is known as Refuse-Derived Fuel (RDF) at the municipal site. Alternatively, it could be collected from people's homes and local collection points where it has already been separated. This separated paper can then be burned as a fuel and thus can be considered as a waste-to-energy technique which improves the value of the waste. Alternatively, it can be viewed as a useful pre-treatment prior to final disposal. All of the thermal methods used are very similar in terms of the underlying physical processes and issues involved.

In most incinerators the waste is burned on moving grates in refractory-lined chambers; the combustible gases and any solids they carry are then burned in secondary chambers. Combustion is normally 85 to 95% complete for the materials that can be burned. In addition to heat, if the newspaper is burned with other combustible materials then the products of incineration can include *carbon dioxide*, water, *oxides of sulphur, oxides of nitrogen*, other gases and smoke. Many of these products are potential harmful environmental pollutants. The non-gaseous products are ash and unburned solid residues. The emission of particulate matter is often controlled by wet scrubbers, *electrostatic precipitators* and filters.

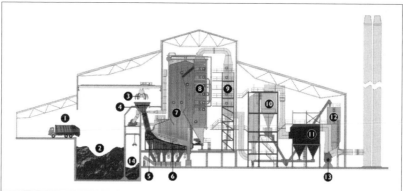

❶ Waste collection vehicle to tip unsorted waste into storage pit

❷ Waste storage pit

❸ Overhead crane to feed waste feeding hopper

❹ Waste feeding hopper

❺ Double movable feeding grate to provide waste to combustion grate

❻ Combustion grate where the waste is burned out

❼ Solidly welded membrane walls fully integrated with the furnace chamber and acting as radiation part of the boiler

❽ Superheater section of the boiler where the final steam temperature is achieved before the steam is sent to the turbine

❾ Economiser section of the boiler where the feed-water coming from the feed-water preparation unit is reheated

❿ Lime scrubber reactor neutralising acid gases contained in the flue gases by lime milk injection

⓫ Particulate matter contained in the flue gases are removed from the gas stream by the baghouse filter

⓬ Silo for collection of residual products: fly ash from boiler and reaction products from reactor and baghouse filter

⓭ Induced draught fan ejecting the clean and dedusted flue gases into the atmosphere via a chimney

⓮ Clinker pit where clinker is transported to collection vehicles alongside the building by an overhead crane. Ferrous metals are recovered by means of a magnetic separator

Figure 4.2 Thermal Treatment - The Teeside Energy From Waste Plant

The burning of your newspaper and other solid materials has four basic objectives. The first is that both its volume and mass are considerably reduced. Typically, the volume reduction can be as much as 90% and the mass reduction 70%. This has major environmental and economic impacts because ash will fill a smaller space in a landfill site and there will be less need for the use of vehicles to transport the waste to the site. The second objective is to reduce the amount of organic matter in the waste thus rendering it less subject to landfill gas formation and leaching. The third is to recover useful heat energy and in doing so reduce the demand on fossil fuel use. Energy derived from waste could provide 3-4% of our energy needs. The fourth objective is to sanitise the waste by destroying potentially dangerous disease causing organisms before the waste is placed in a landfill site. In addition to the destruction of pathogens, efficient heat treatment can destroy chemicals such as dioxins. *Heavy metals*, e.g. *cadmium*, are also concentrated in the ashes and clinker in quantities which could be harmful to the biosphere. These should be found in the form of their *oxides* which effectively reduces the availability of the metals because the oxides are not very soluble in water.

The environmental impact of thermal treatment has shown and continues to show itself in a number of ways. Firstly in order to incinerate any solid waste, fuel is needed to start up and continue the process of incineration. Hence efficient as well as effective incinerators need to be used to lower the demands on non-renewable energy resources. The second factor is the emission of pollutants to the atmosphere via the flue gases. The burning of your newspaper alone would produce carbon dioxide gas, water vapour and possibly smoke particles which will enter the environment via the flue. Whilst the emission of pollutants is now physically and legally carefully controlled in all developed countries, in the past there have been some serious cases of the continual expulsion to the atmosphere of hazardous by-products of burning, e.g. the *dioxins*. These latter chemicals, though, are highly unlikely to be derived from your newspaper!

The **biological treatment** of solid waste (cf. Figure 4.3) uses naturally occurring micro-organisms to decompose its *biodegradable* components. These components are derived from plant and animal materials including your newspaper. Household waste typically contains between 20% to 60% of this kind of material. There are two basic ways of decomposing organic material. One involves *aerobic* treatment and the other *anaerobic* treatment. Aerobic treatment is usually called **composting**, whilst anaerobic treatment is often referred to as anaerobic fermentation/digestion or **biogasification**. Composting is very familiar to the gardener, but on the large scale biodegradable material must be collected at centralised biological treatment plants. The type of initial treatment that takes place depends upon the origin of the organic matter. Household waste would require extensive separation techniques ranging from hand sorting to the use of electromagnets to remove ferrous based metals. If the organic matter has been separated at source it is called Biowaste, VGF (vegetable, fruit and garden) and green wastes. This latter material would require no expensive separation at the plant before treatment. Under aerobic conditions, the products are

Green waste is delivered to site for processing (thus reducing solid waste going to landfill).

Green waste is shredded after checking for unwanted contamination.

Shredded waste is formed into wind rows approximately 2.5m high x 3.5m wide and allowed to decompose under aerobic conditions for at least 6 months.

After sieving the compacted material is bagged for sale.

Figure 4.3 Biological Treatment - Scarborough B.C. Organic Green Compost Process

carbon dioxide, water vapour and compost. Heat is also produced, i.e. the process of decomposition is exothermic. In the case of anaerobic conditions, methane gas, carbon dioxide, water vapour and an organic residue are produced. The latter may be useful as a compost.

What then are the objectives of such biological treatment and the environmental consequences? When used as a pre-treatment it firstly helps to reduce the volume of the waste via loss of material in the form of carbon dioxide, water vapour and methane gas. The loss of water in particular is useful because it can help to lessen the amount of leachate should the reduced material be placed in a landfill site. Secondly, pre-treatment helps to stabilise the waste because it would be less subject to biological decomposition and therefore a better landfill material. Thirdly, in the case of composting in particular, it is an effective way of sanitising the waste because the aerobic temperatures developed destroy the majority of *pathogens* and seeds that may be present. However, the composting process consumes more energy than it produces. The energy produced is not even in a useful form and thus this process causes a net loss of useful energy from the environment. However, composting does replace other threatened materials such as peat based composts.

Anaerobic conditions are mildly exothermic but the waste can be warmed by the application of external heat to a temperature that sterilises the waste. A major aim of biogasification is the production of compost and a fuel known as biogas which contains a high percentage of methane. The biogas can be stored easily, burned on site to provide electricity or sold and delivered elsewhere. Biogasification consumes energy during the process but the production of a fuel means that there is a net gain in useful energy. The compost produced by both processes can be usefully used to improve the quality of soil and act as a fertiliser. The major drawback is that the origin of the solid waste giving rise to the compost needs to be carefully monitored so that the compost sold does not contain a dangerous level of hazardous materials.

All methods of handling solid waste can result in the removal of recyclable materials before the process is started, during its operation and at its end. If we return to the case of the newspaper, the obvious thing to do with it would be to place it in a "paper bank" from where it could be recycled after appropriate treatment elsewhere. However, if the newspaper had to be carried in the back of a car to a local central collecting point, the environmental costs incurred could be more than the value of the recyclable paper. Couple this with the atmospheric pollution caused by the running of the motor vehicle and the use of the fuel, then one could ask the question whether sorting at source is sensible. Whatever the material is that is to be recycled, the drive to do so is often based just on economic criteria and market demands. The cost of energy consumption in the transport of recyclable material to a treatment centre and in its processing need to be balanced against the same costs involved in using virgin material. Recycling may appear to "save the environment and save resources" but it does involve a balancing act of resource versus energy. If nothing else, perhaps the encouragement of recycling such things as aluminium cans, glass containers and paper makes the public more aware of the need to conserve resources.

FACT FILE 4.1

PETROL is also called gasoline and is a major *hydrocarbon* fuel. It is a mixture containing mainly *hexane*, *octane* and *heptane*. Most modern car engines have high compression ratio engines and the mixture of air and petrol vapour supplied to it can prematurely explode, pushing against a rising instead of a descending piston. This is called "knocking" and to eliminate it many petroleum manufacturers have added *tetraethyl lead* and *dibromoethane* as anti-knocking agents to prevent early detonation. When leaded petrol is burned it produces a number of waste products which are exhausted to our atmosphere. Amongst these "car fumes" are *carbon dioxide*, *carbon monoxide*, *nitrogen oxides*, unburned hydrocarbons, water vapour, *hydrobromic acid*, and a *volatile* compound of lead called *lead dibromide*. Carbon monoxide is a toxic gas, hydrobromic acid corrodes exhaust systems and lead dibromide has been blamed for affecting the central nervous system of growing children.

FACT FILE 4.2

HAZARDOUS WASTES cause problems because they are often non-degradable and persistent in nature. Their effects can be magnified by living organisms which can, for example, concentrate heavy metals in their tissues. Such waste is often lethal if sufficient quantities are absorbed via the respiratory system or digestive system of humans. Often they can be detrimental over long periods of time. Hazardous wastes can include toxic chemicals, radioactive materials, biological materials and flammable substances. They can take any physical form, including sludges.

RADON is a naturally occurring, radioactive, colourless, odourless gas found in very small quantities in the Earth's atmosphere. It is produced by the natural radioactive decay of uranium minerals found in some rocks and soil. Radon is the main contributor to background or natural radiation. Normally it is harmless unless it becomes concentrated in, for example, spaces beneath floorboards, particularly in buildings built in granite rock regions. In certain parts of Great Britain some houses have to be specially ventilated to prevent the build-up of this gas. Radioactive substances are hazardous because prolonged exposure to their radiation can cause serious damage to cells. Solid radioactive wastes are normally not important potential contaminants of the environment unless they become airborne or waterborne by leaching.

EUTROPHICATION is a process by which a body of water becomes rich in inorganic nutrients by run-off from farmland and other artificial means. Compounds containing potassium, phosphorus, nitrogen, iron and sulphur are vital for plant growth in water. However, if present in excess amounts they can over-stimulate the growth of plants, algae and micro-organisms.

CHLOROFLUOROCARBONS or **CFCs** are compounds of chlorine, fluorine and carbon. A typical example is Freon 11 which has the molecular formula CCl_3F. Freon 11 is/was used as an aerosol propellant, refrigerant and as a blowing agent for foam plastics.

They are chemically very stable, unreactive gases and volatile liquids. When they are released into the atmosphere they rise and eventually reach the ozone layer. Here they are broken down by the ultraviolet radiation from the sun to form chlorine monoxide. This substance acts as a catalyst in the breaking down of ozone into oxygen. One molecule of chlorine monoxide, because it itself remains unchanged, can enable the breakdown of thousands of ozone molecules.

Further Reading Chapter 4

Ash Handling from Waste Combustion, Technical Information Sheet, The World Resource Foundation, Tonbridge, c1995

R.E. Hester & R.M. Harrison (Eds), *Waste Incineration & the Environment*, Cambridge, Royal Society of Chemistry, 1994

R.E. Hester & R.M. Harrison (Eds), *Waste Treatment & Disposal*, Cambridge, Royal Society of Chemistry, 1995

Landfill Mining, Technical Information Sheet, The World Resource Foundation, Tonbridge, c1995

Landfill Techniques, Technical Information Sheet, The World Resource Foundation, Tonbridge, c1995

K.Martin & T.W. Bastock (Eds), *Waste Minimisation: A Chemist's Approach*, Cambridge, Royal Society of Chemistry, 1994

Materials Reclamation Facilities, Technical Information Sheet, The World Resource Foundation, Tonbridge, c1995

CHAPTER 5

SOLID WASTES
an integrated approach to their management

The objectives of solid waste management are described. The reasons why an integrated waste management system is needed are discussed, and the terminology of Life Cycle Assessment explained. The Life Cycle Assessment approach is applied to the sorting and collection of domestic waste. Suggestions are made as to how you can help to reduce the environmental impact of solid waste.

INTRODUCTION

So far much has been written about the need to ensure personal and environmental safety; the importance of making sure that we can sustain the availability of resources via effective and efficient usage, and the need for an integrated approach to environmental management. Having already identified what we mean by solid waste and the different ways in which they are dealt with, we will now look at how such waste can be managed so that all of these factors are taken into account.

The key concept involved is "sustainable development", i.e. helping to ensure that your needs are met without compromising the needs of future generations. Industry can help to meet society's needs by attempting to produce more value from goods and services with less consumption of the world's resources and the production of less pollution - the "more from less" approach. Indeed, this has been carried out very successfully in a number of initiatives, e.g. the improvement of packaging to provide lightweight and refillable packaging. These initiatives have generally increased customer satisfaction, as well as leading to a decrease in the burden on the environment in terms of both emissions and the use of material and energy resources.

The same approach can be adopted in the management of solid waste. Solid waste management should contribute to environmental sustainability and use the "more for less" approach. It must enable the **recovery** of materials and energy, i.e. more value from waste, the **consumption** of less materials and energy, the **release** of less emissions, and a minimal loss of amenities. In this chapter, we outline the use of the Life Cycle Inventory approach in assessing how well a particular system performs, and propose that Integrated (Solid) Waste Management offers the best potential for achieving sustainability.

THE OBJECTIVES OF SOLID WASTE MANAGEMENT

When energy and raw materials are taken from the environment and used in, say, an industrial process, waste is produced that ultimately finds its way to landfill (cf. Fig.5.1a). By including some method of waste prevention, less energy and raw materials will be required to complete that process and less waste will be produced (cf. Fig.5.1b). If an integrated waste management approach is adopted then energy and materials may be recovered and used to supplement both the energy and raw materials input stream. This would reduce even further the initial energy and raw materials demands and the amount of waste produced (cf. Fig.5.1c).

As indicated in earlier chapters, no matter what the process is there will always be waste and this has to be managed. Thus, two of the major objectives of solid waste management are to reduce the overall amounts of energy and raw materials required, and the amount of waste produced by a process. This is the cornerstone of

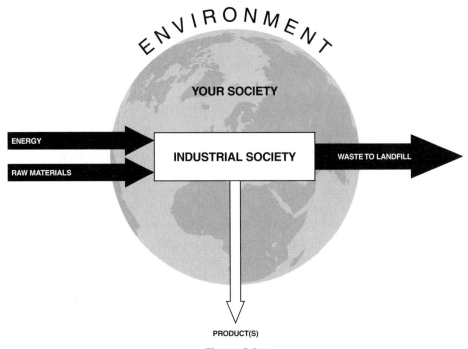

Figure 5.1a

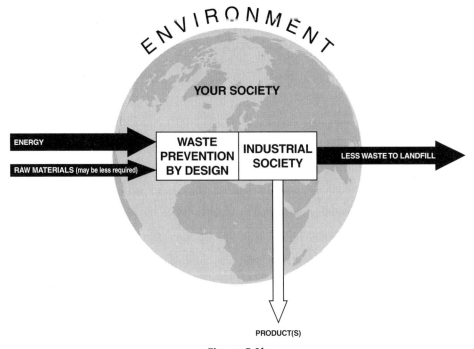

Figure 5.1b

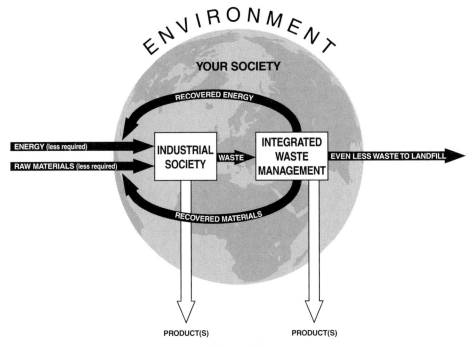

Figure 5.1c

environmental sustainability, which demands a reduction in the overall environmental impacts of waste management, including the reduction of energy consumption and emission of pollutants, in a **cost-effective** way. In other words, any environmental improvements that can be achieved will be sustainable in the long term only if they are financially viable. The cost needs to be acceptable to the society that the waste management serves, including businesses, governments and all of us as private citizens. Costs will vary according to where the waste is generated, but providing that they are similar to existing costs for the collection and disposal of waste then this should be acceptable to most people. In the UK, domestic waste disposal is charged at a flat rate - there is thus currently no economic incentive for the householder to bother reducing waste. In countries where charging has been introduced, e.g. the USA, Canada, Korea and Germany, the amounts of waste produced by households have been considerably reduced. One problem that might occur as a result of high "waste fees" could be unauthorised dumping. Certainly this continues to be a problem with industrial and commercial waste. In the UK in May 1998, the Environmental Agency was investigating two examples of illegal dumping in North Yorkshire. The first involved the dumping of about three tons of asbestos-based material on a grass verge in the countryside near the town of Malton. The second investigation concerned the dumping of hazardous medical waste at a civic amenity tip near Whitby. Here about 1000 used syringes, 100 glass phials of anaesthetic, used scalpels and medicines obtainable only by prescription were amongst the items found in a skip. There will always, it appears, be conflict between the cost of collecting and treating waste, and environmental impact. It is probable that deciding between these two variables will always be the source of problems, worries and heated debate.

How then can solid waste be managed? The answer to this question will depend upon both the quantity and composition of the solid waste produced. For example, it has been estimated that a total of about 1600 million tonnes of solid waste is produced each year in Europe. Much of this is agricultural, mining and dredging waste and is disposed of at source. The rest of the waste amounts to about 530 million tonnes, which has to be treated. Of this latter figure, about 106 million tonnes are classified as municipal waste, which contains household and commercial material. A mean value of about 350-kg per year of municipal waste is generated for each person living in Europe. It is though worth noting that statistics on waste are still generally poor and there is much room for improvement. There is also a wide variation in what is called "municipal solid waste". Table 5.1 gives a typical composition of this very complex mixture. This composition varies from country to country and within a country, e.g. from North to South France.

Table 5.1 Composition of European Municipal Solid Waste.

TYPE OF MATERIAL	PERCENTAGE COMPOSITION BY MASS	TYPE OF MATERIAL	PERCENTAGE COMPOSITION BY MASS
Food/Garden	39	Metals	5
Paper & Board	25	Textiles	1
Plastic	7	Others	15
Glass	8	-	-

Examination of Table 5.1 will show that, excluding food and garden waste, potentially around 45% by mass of the waste could be recovered for the recycling of materials, 64% could be composted (food/garden, paper and board) and 71% could be usefully incinerated (food/garden, paper and board, plastics). However, the choice of waste disposal method is not as simple as these figures suggest. For example, it would make little environmental or economic sense to try to recover all of the paper and plastic for recycling since much of it will be too small or too dirty to be used. An additional problem is that different materials will need to be treated in different ways. There is no single waste treatment process which alone can manage all waste materials in an environmentally sensitive way. Thus, an integrated approach is needed which involves a range of waste management options capable of dealing with the different fractions within solid waste. Such an approach is outlined in the following sections.

INTEGRATED WASTE MANAGEMENT

For an Integrated Waste strategy to work and achieve all of the above objectives requires, as the first step, an effective system of collecting and sorting. This should result in waste in sufficient quantities and in well-defined piles suitable for subsequent treatment by a range of methods. After this initial sorting, the different groups of waste can be treated according to the materials they contain. Treatment can include a complementary rather than competing combination of methods which include recycling of materials, biological treatment of organic matter (biogasification and composting), thermal treatment (mass burning of domestic waste, packaging-derived fuel and refuse-derived fuel) and landfilling of the inert residues. Recovering of energy from the waste can occur in several of these options including biological treatment (biogasification), thermal treatment (burning as fuel or recovering energy from domestic solid waste incineration) and land filling (recovering landfill gas). Recycling, composting and converting waste to energy depend upon the economic situation of the markets for their respective outputs.

The main elements of Integrated Waste Management are shown in Fig.5.2.

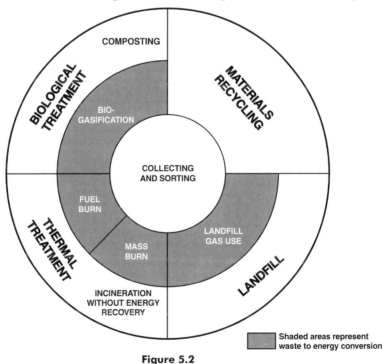

Figure 5.2

The system is described as integrated since it takes an overall approach and **combines** a range of waste treatment methods, and handles a range of different **types** of materials. Such a system should be capable of handing the waste arising not just from municipal solid waste but also from a number of different **sources**. Integrated Waste Management also offers flexibility in the choice and operations of its systems according to prevailing social, economic and environmental conditions. For example, paper can be recycled, composted or incinerated according to supply and demand for paper. If consistency in quantity and quality of useful waste is required, together with the need to apply a range of disposal methods and the economy normally associated with scale, then a large scale, regionally organised waste disposal approach would be required.

Currently, in the UK, because of the way in which solid waste collection and disposal is organised and dispersed between public and private sectors, it can be difficult to use an integrated approach. Indeed, it is often impossible to identify any single person who has control over our waste management. This should not, though, dissuade us from investigating and putting into practice Integrated Waste Management.

The use of an Integrated Waste Management approach would give a much more precise overall view of waste management which can be invaluable for strategic planning. In addition, a more global picture of the impact of wastes on the ecosystem would evolve, and a clearer economic picture and assessment would be obtained. Perhaps the way forward in some areas is to start afresh and design a new system of waste management where all methods of disposal are interconnected. Economic efficiencies may well be discovered that will help to offset the cost of this new approach.

Since solid waste management must be both environmentally and economically sustainable, how can we predict both the environmental impacts and the overall economic costs of this management? Given that there are a number of possible combinations of waste treatment methods, how can we compare both the economic and environmental performance of different Integrated Waste Management systems? In the past, solid waste treatment has been managed on the basis of a placing the options available in a preferred order and then proceeding through that order. As seen in Chapter 4, this order has often taken the form of waste minimisation, the re-use of waste, the recycling/biological treatment of materials, thermal treatment and finally landfilling. Unfortunately, the outcomes of proceeding through such an order have not always proved to be advantageous to our environment.

In recent years, a new environmental management tool called **Life Cycle Assessment (LCA)** has been developing which tries to predict and compare the environmental impacts of a product, process or service from its "birth/cradle" to its "death/grave". In the case of a product, LCA examines every stage of its life cycle from the winning of raw materials from the earth itself, through the manufacture, distribution, use, possible re-use/recycling and final disposal. For each stage, the inputs of raw materials and energy and the emissions to air, water and landfill are calculated. (This latter step is an accounting process and is called the **Life Cycle Inventory**.) The calculations from each stage are then aggregated over the entire life cycle. The inputs and outputs are converted into their effects on the environment, i.e. their environmental impacts. The sum of these environmental impacts represents the overall environmental effects of the life cycle being investigated. Hence, LCA considers much more than just one environmental issue. If LCA modelling is carried out for alternative products, processes or services, then fair comparisons can be made concerning their environmental impacts. If one turns out to be better than the others and is financially viable then its selection may lead to environmental improvement. This tool has increasingly been applied to the management of solid waste.

LIFE CYCLE ASSESSMENT AND THE MANAGEMENT OF SOLID WASTE

In order to understand Life Cycle Assessment (LCA) as it is applied to solid waste, it is first necessary to explain the term "life cycle". In the case of solid waste, the collection and delivery of that waste to the starting point in its treatment may be described as its "birth". The rest of its life can then be described in terms of the treatment it might undergo before its "death" and final interment in the graveyard of the land fill site. LCA then becomes the tool by which the effectiveness of the solid waste management system being used can be evaluated. If an Integrated Waste Management system is seen as being enclosed by an imaginary boundary wall, then what goes into the system from its surroundings and what is put back into the surroundings in terms of both energy and materials can be easily identified. Thus, the assessment of the environmental impacts of the passage of matter and energy to and from the environment can be attempted. Just as in the case of a product, the LCA methodology used enables different modifications to the waste management system, and indeed different systems, to be compared from the point of view of energy and materials use, environmental impact of gaseous, liquid and solid emissions and relative costs.

How then is a LCA of an integrated waste management system performed? The assessment is generally considered to be comprised of three main stages. These are **goal definition**, taking an **inventory**, and the **interpretation** of that inventory in terms of environmental impact.

The first very important stage involves defining what your goals or aims are, i.e. goal definition. In this stage the boundaries of what is being investigated are clearly defined and this, in turn, allows the identification of what is to be left out and included in any subsequent collection and analysis of data. Boundary definition can be as simple as the real fencing around a factory, or an imaginary boundary around a whole set of interrelated waste treatment methods. Usually where the treatment of waste is involved in goal definition then the types and forms of waste are identified, together with all the options available for its treatment.

The second stage requires the collection of data, i.e. an inventory, which lists all the material and energy inputs and outputs over the whole lifetime of the waste management process. As indicated earlier, in order to do this, the life cycle is broken down into a series of steps, and the material and energy inputs and outputs are calculated for each step. The results from each step then form a separate list of material and energy inputs, together with corresponding emissions to air and water, and solid waste. Individual results are then combined in some way to give an overall idea of, for example, how much energy will be needed to treat the waste or how much material will be going to landfill.

The third stage is the interpretation of the information obtained from the inventory stage. It is by the careful assessment of this data that conclusions may be reached about the overall burden the environment will carry (environmental impact) as a consequence of operating the system. This is a much more difficult stage than just making a set of lists because of the subjective nature of some of the information and the need to make objective judgements. One way of determining environmental impact is to collect all emissions from all of the steps under headings such as emissions to air, emissions to water, and production of solid waste, and then weight the emissions in some way according to their toxicity. The results can then be added to give a total effect. However, such an approach is not without its faults. How, for example, do you compare the effects on the environment of burning waste to produce energy, which predominantly produces emissions to air, with the landfilling of waste which involves air and water pollution as well as transport impacts? Individual pollutants in emissions to air, for example, can contribute to a range of different environmental problems, such as ozone depletion, global warming and acid-rain formation as well as having their own individual toxicity. Indeed, aggregating the effects of a waste material under any one heading can also present problems; for example, organic waste materials in landfill sites can affect soil, air and water.

Probably the most meaningful way of determining environmental impact is to aggregate emissions according to their effects on the environment. For example, all the emissions to air from various points within a waste management system that contribute to ozone depletion can be aggregated together, and each can be weighted according to their relative contribution to the environmental problem. However this is done, the overall result should reflect the contribution of the life cycle of the waste to a set of identified environmental problems.

Although there has been general agreement about some aspects of each of the three stages involved in LCA, there is as yet no complete approach. It continues to be a developing science.

The goal definition and inventory stages have both been used to help in the management of solid waste in a number of countries including the USA, Canada, Spain and the UK. Case studies showing how life cycle inventory studies have been used in planning waste management are now beginning to appear. In the past such studies have often focused on environmental factors only, but an integrated waste management system also needs to be economically sustainable.

The general system boundaries, inputs and outputs for the life cycle inventory study of solid waste are shown in Figure 5.3. As can be seen, in addition to the waste itself, there are energy and other material inputs (e.g. petrol, diesel) to the system. Some of the outputs are useful products in the form of reclaimed materials and compost, but others are emissions to air and water and inert landfill material. Energy will also be produced in waste to energy options, e.g. use of recovered landfill gas, which when combined with the energy inputs to the system will give a value for the overall energy consumption. It must be remembered that not only is energy in the form of petrol, diesel, gas or electricity expended in the treatment of waste, energy is also expended in the extraction and production of these fuel sources. These latter processes will also have contributed to emissions to air and water, and solid waste. The impacts of energy production by the energy industries can also be legitimately included in any energy calculations involved in a life cycle inventory. Calculations concerning the costs involved should be carried out in parallel with energy and material investigations. Economic costs of a waste management system, i.e. what has to be paid for, will include collection, sorting, various forms of treatment, transport and final disposal to landfill. Income from the system will come from the sale of reclaimed materials, compost and energy. Subtracting the income from costs will give an indication of the net cost of operating such a system. When considering the overall economic costs the purchasing of capital equipment, e.g. vehicles and incinerators, and their depreciation must also be part of the calculation.

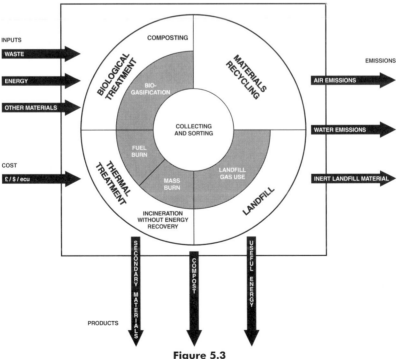

Figure 5.3

As indicated earlier, the inventory stage establishes all inputs and outputs in the life cycle of solid waste. The first step is to define the life cycle. Since the main objective of a Life Cycle Inventory tool should be to describe the majority of waste management systems, existing or planned, all processes and combinations of processes need to be possible. The main stages in the life cycle of solid waste, and their interconnections, are shown in a simplified way in Figure 5.4. The stages are pre-sorting and collection, central sorting, biological treatment, thermal treatment and landfilling. Once each stage is established, then the processes within a stage can be identified, and all energy and material inputs and outputs listed. By linking up all processes within each stage and then all the stages in a lifecycle, it is possible to define the overall waste management system. How this may be done will be illustrated later with respect to the pre-sorting and collection stage.

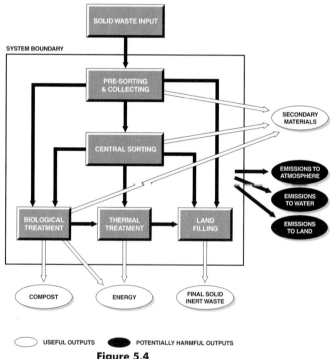

Figure 5.4

A life cycle inventory for solid waste management consists, then, of two main steps. Firstly, the waste management system to be considered must be described and its boundaries defined. This involves choosing between the different possible waste treatment options. Secondly, the inputs and outputs of the chosen process must be calculated from the best available information, which itself is dependent upon the performance of the equipment and technologies available. Currently, the lack of quality data is a major problem in any life cycle inventory of solid waste, but efforts are underway by the US Environmental Protection Agency and UK Environmental Agency to remedy this situation.

PRE-SORTING AND THE COLLECTION OF SOLID WASTE

A total picture of a lifecycle inventory for solid waste is beyond the scope of this book. It is instructive, though, to analyse just one of the processes involved, that of the pre-sorting and collection of solid waste. From the point of view of most of us, the pre-sorting and collection of waste is normally our only point of contact with the waste management system. How this initial process is carried out will dictate to a very large extent how the waste will ultimately be treated and whether methods intended to add value to the waste (valorisation), such as fuel burning and materials recycling, are feasible in an economical and environmentally sustainable way. Collection methods will significantly influence the quality of recovered materials, compost or fuel that can be produced. Market demand for reclaimed materials will also define how they are sorted and collected. In 1998, for example, in Ireland the Dublin kerbside collection scheme had not collected newspapers, magazines and other waste paper for two years because of the zero or negative price of this kind of waste.

Let us start at your home and your own rubbish! Although you may think otherwise, your dustbin is not necessarily the grave of your waste. Waste only becomes waste when it finally ceases to have any value. Thus in the context of the management of waste, the "cradle" of your waste is the dustbin. Household and similar commercial waste is either collected (the dustbin men) or delivered (e.g. to a bottle bank) in a variety of ways. Here, for you, it is easy to identify a very practical example of a boundary, i.e. the point at which it leaves your house or commercial property. What you do to reduce the amount of waste at this point reduces the amount to be collected. The "grave" of your waste is when it is finally deposited back into the environment, i.e. when the waste becomes inert landfill material or becomes emissions to air or water.

Most householders need to have their waste collected with the minimum of inconvenience in terms of the effort needed, time taken and the space that is occupied by waste collection containers. On the other hand, the collector wants the waste in a form compatible with planned disposal methods. Clearly there is a need to balance these competing needs if a waste management system is to be successful. The collection system will also dictate to what extent additional value can be obtained from waste. If some value is to be obtained from your waste then some form of separation of that waste into different fractions at source, i.e. your home, prior to collection would be necessary. What you are willing to do will depend upon your ability to separate waste and the motivation that you work under. Anyone's willingness to separate waste will be greatly enhanced by clear guidance on how to do it properly. There are many people who are motivated by their regard for and worries about the environment, and so would respond very positively to guidance. For example, a study in Leeds, UK, showed that it was possible for volunteers (the well motivated!) to sort their waste into six different categories with a 96.5% success rate. Participation rates in other voluntary sorting studies have also shown high success

Rubbish:
A typical local amenity tip
(the low hill in the
background is made of
rubbish)

Rubbish:
Impossible to sort

Rubbish:
In the street

Figure 5.5 A Typical Local Amenity Tip (Photos taken by the author)

rates. If householders received a reduction in charges for their waste removal as a result of pre-sorting their waste then perhaps participation rates throughout a country would be high? Some countries go further than this, and the separation of certain fractions of waste at source is a legal requirement. Certainly, motivation is a key factor in getting people to participate in a collection scheme and in achieving good separation efficiency. Even if pre-sorting becomes a matter of law, its effectiveness will depend upon the level of convenience. There will always be problems if too much time is involved in the sorting process or too much space is taken up by "specialised" containers, or offensive smells build up as a result of irregular collections.

There are two basic ways that collection can occur. The first we will label "bring" collecting and the second "kerbside" collecting.

In the case of "bring" collecting, you take the waste to a collection point, e.g. bottles to a bottle bank or garden waste to the "local tip" or civic amenity. Waste has thus been pre-sorted by the householder, or may in turn go on to be centrally sorted. (How many readers of this book have been to a local tip and not paid any attention to requests concerning where to put your various types of rubbish?) This kind of collecting is heavily dependent on you supplying your own transport, but makes a lower demand on transport by the collector. The amount of different kinds of waste collected varies from low to high because it depends upon the population of people feeding the collection point. The kind of waste collected can be of low to high quality in terms of how well the materials are initially separated and whether or not they remain so at the collection point.

The "kerbside" method consists of you placing your waste in a containers for collection in the immediate vicinity of your property and the containers being collected for you. The waste can be sorted by you before collection or it may be sorted at the kerbside and/or centrally. You are not dependent on transport for this but there is a high dependency on transport on the part of the collector. It is clear that in both methods transport costs and the effects of the vehicles themselves on the environment must be taken into account. The amount collected is high, providing that the motivation is there. Cross contamination of the sorted waste is high if a mixed collection takes place, but is low if more than one collection container is supplied to the householder. This is sometimes referred to as a "Blue Box" situation (c.f. Fact File 5.1 for an example case study.). From the above, we can now place the pre-sorting and collecting stage within an integrated waste management system (c.f. Figure 5.6.).

Environmental Impact Analysis

If the Life Cycle Inventory is a good one, then it is possible to obtain details concerning energy consumption, materials consumption, emissions, and solid waste production which could be very useful in aiding management decisions concerning

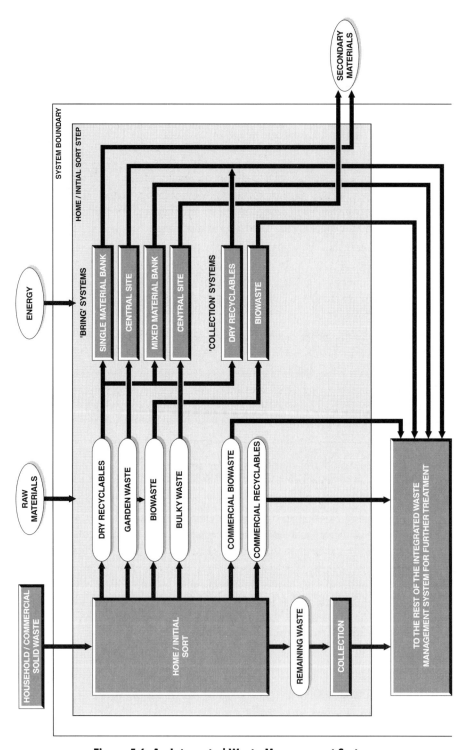

Figure 5.6 An Integrated Waste Management System

waste management. LCA could also be very important in controlling costs. However, environmental impact data for waste management is far from being complete. There is, for example, much more data available concerning the emissions from incinerators than on landfilling.

An approach that has been adopted in trying to quantify environmental impact begins by identifying some environmental categories that are associated, for example, with the treatment of one tonne of collected waste. These categories are of global, continental or regional importance. Energy resource depletion can be reflected in the total energy consumed and can be a global or local category. Global categories include greenhouse gas emissions (carbon dioxide, methane, nitrous oxide) and acid gas emissions (nitrogen oxides, sulphur dioxide, hydrogen chloride). Continental or regional categories include chemicals that cause smogs (nitrogen oxides), air emissions that contain heavy metals and trace organic compounds, and emissions to water of heavy metals, trace organic materials and those causing heavy biological oxygen demand. The final local/regional category for the environment is the management of the residual solid waste. Thus, the results from the treatment of solid waste can be listed under each of these problem areas. It should be remembered that when dealing with global issues such as resource depletion, global warming, ozone depletion, and so on, the exact site and time of emissions is not important since all sites affect the global ecosystem.

If, for example, we wanted to know what the environmental impact might be as a result of trying to recover energy in the form of waste incineration, then the exact nature of the incineration process would need to be known. Typical emission values and associated problems for waste incinerators are well documented. Thus, heavy metal concentrations in the ash, and the various types and quantities of emissions to air and water can be estimated. Greenhouse gas calculations can be based on the carbon content of the waste.

The overall environmental impact that must be considered in a cost versus impact analysis needs to include local as well as global environments. Local impacts are especially important when dealing with emissions to air and particularly to water. Here knowledge such as toxicity and persistence of materials is essential, as well as when and how they were released.

The Life Cycle Inventory involves an integration process of aggregating and weighting emissions over various sites over time. It is not, therefore, applicable to local impact measurements. Local environmental impact requires a review of raw data at a site and the determination of hazards involved and the risks that they pose. This requires knowledge of the fate of materials, levels of exposure and dose effects (c.f. Chapter 2). Risk analysis is then followed by risk assessment, thus leading to predictions about local environmental impact.

You and Waste from Your Home

One of the main advantages of using an Integrated Waste Management approach to solid waste is that it is possible to help identify where improvements can be made in the handling of that waste. Taking a Life Cycle Inventory of solid waste can improve the process of monitoring the performance of waste management and help in making a more effective choice between the different waste treatment options.

Can we, as householders, help to improve what we do with our waste? In order to identify where it may be possible to make the greatest improvements, we must first identify where the largest impacts occur, and then determine ways of reducing them. This involves a careful analysis of the system being investigated, to show where changes can be made which will result in significant improvements. If environmental impacts are reduced by what is done, then this will mean that there has been an overall improvement in the waste system. It is perhaps much more obvious to the householder how improvements can be made when dealing with something like a landfill site. It is clear, for example, that if more landfill gas were collected and burned with the consequent recovery of energy, or more landfill sites were lined thus containing leachate, then there would be less potentially harmful emissions to air and water. It may not be so obvious what can be done by the householder or commercial waste producer to improve solid waste management.

As indicated earlier in this chapter, the way in which the householder behaves is vitally important in the overall management of solid waste. If your solid waste was simply collected as unsorted waste and transported directly to a landfill site without further treatment, then what you do is easy to see. You simply fill your bin, allow it to be collected, and let others worry about the outcomes. If you were to pre-sort recyclable materials and make a special trip, say of about one mile each way, to a materials bank each week, then there would be a very large increase in the overall energy consumed in the treatment of waste. If you were asked to use an extra plastic collection bag to put recyclable materials in then it would again result in a large extra consumption of energy to make the bag. If you were to separate biological degradable materials from the rest of your domestic waste then it is likely that you would want to wash out the bin each month using warm water, yet again increasing the energy consumed. Clearly, the actions of the householder coupled with the pre-sorting of waste are very important since their collective result on energy consumption alone can be very dramatic.

You can reduce the amount of solid waste you produce in a number of ways. You can choose to use, for example, concentrated or compact products that contribute less waste themselves, and use less packaging per use. Using refill packs or light-weight containers can reduce household waste significantly. Reduction in waste can also be achieved by buying goods in appropriate amounts and sizes. How many of us have thrown away that half-filled can of paint because we bought a tin too large for the job? How many of us throw away food because we bought too much to be eaten before it became stale? If the householder were to generate less solid waste then the overall environmental impacts caused by total waste management systems would fall. You can of course give as much added value as possible to your waste by agreeing to sort the waste effectively into appropriate categories.

Domestic waste is one of the most difficult of all wastes to deal with in an environmentally friendly and economic way. The householder must be involved in its management in a way that provides improvements in the quality of the environment, helps to reduce demand on energy and material resources, as well as reducing the volume of waste. This can only be done if householders are convinced that waste management is advantageous to them and that it is being done by others as effectively and efficiently as possible. Information and encouragement by waste managers must be provided to ensure this. At the earliest stage possible, the education of our children must include not just the importance of saving animals and plants but of also reducing solid waste, particularly municipal waste.

FACT FILE 5.1
A Kerbside Collection Scheme, Adur District, West Sussex, UK

In May 1991, a so-called "Blue Box" dry recyclable collection scheme was started in Adur District, West Middlesex, UK. Here a blue box of capacity 44 litres was supplied to householders living in low-rise suburban housing. These boxes were set out by the householder at the kerbside when full of dry recyclable materials, The boxes were collected once a week by a special multi-compartment vehicle. The box contents were sorted by the operator at the vehicle into five categories: green glass, brown glass, clear glass, paper and plastic containers and film, metal (iron and aluminium) cans. All other waste was collected weekly by normal refuse vehicles. In addition to this, close-to-home drop-off centres were supplied for those homes not covered by the Blue Box scheme. 19500 households were covered by the Blue Box Scheme. 6500 households had access to the close-to-home drop-off points. It was found that there was a 75% participation rate among Blue Box householders. 129 kg of recyclable materials out of a total waste stream of 460 kg were collected from each participant per year. It was estimated in 1992 that the additional collection cost of the recyclable materials was £17.60 per household per year, as opposed to £35.00 per household per year for the collection of the residual waste. This additional cost subsequently fell to £5.00, then to £1.33 per household and today there is no added cost.

Further Reading Chapter 5

Open University Course team, *Municipal Solid Waste Management*, T237, Units 8-9 Environmental Control & Public Health, Milton Keynes, Open University press, 1993.

Waste matters - Good Practice in Waste Management, London, Audit Commission, 1998.

Dublin Waste Plan-Regional & Integrated, *Walmer Bulletin, Journal of the World Resource Foundation*, May 1998, No.60.

K.K.Westlake, *Landfill Waste Pollution & Control*, Chichester, Albion, 1995.

P.White et al, *Integrated Solid Waste Management; A Lifecycle Inventory*, London, Blackie Academic & Professional, 1994.

CHAPTER 6

WASTE WATER, TYPHUS & CHOLERA
heptonstall slack and london's big stink

A 19th Century village water supply and sewage system is described in order to explain what can happen if sewage and drinking water are mixed and the correct treatments not carried out. The nature of sewage and how it is treated in a modern sewage plant are described. The ways in which water can become polluted and how our drinking water is purified are explained.

WATER SUPPLY AND SEWAGE TREATMENT

After using a toilet have you ever thought of where everything goes and what happens to it? Have you ever thought of where your drinking water comes from? At a first glance, these two questions may seem totally unrelated but as you will see the quality of your drinking water may well depend on the effectiveness of how your sewage is treated.

The more sophisticated people become, the more water they seem to need. Whilst it is true that domestic demand for clean, safe, water in the developed countries is increasing, it is far outweighed by the demands of industry and agriculture. Although water is the most plentiful natural resource and is in constant circulation (cf. Fig 6.1), the demand for water often exceeds the local natural supply and therefore it often has to be transported from somewhere else and purified if necessary. In addition to natural sources of water, treated (and untreated) waste water can also become part of our water supply. Most modern sewage treatment systems are very effective in cleaning up waste water, which can then be returned to a river or lake. The quality of our water supply can be closely linked to the sewage system since the outflow of that system is sometimes connected to the very source of our drinking water. In many parts of Great Britain which have experienced large population growths, it has become necessary to re-use treated water from rivers downstream from the outflow pipes of the sewage works. Currently about 30% of all drinking water supplies in Great Britain involve indirect re-use.

Wherever man has permanently established himself, he has always had the problem of getting rid of his own organic wastes or sewage and sometimes that of his domestic animals. Mother Nature disposes of organic waste matter in four main ways - by dilution, oxidation, putrefaction and filtration. Before the Industrial Revolution and the development of large towns and cities, people relied upon these natural processes and generally dumped their sewage in fields. Here its water content would seep through the soil and thus be filtered and purified. When it rained the solids were eventually dissolved and oxidised and became part of the natural nutrients of the soil.

As soon as there is any increase in population then this reliance on nature does not work. In early Rome, for example, a system of aqueducts was built (between 312 BC and 226 AD) to enable sewage to be borne away by water into the River Tiber. The Romans thus used the Tiber to dilute their sewage. Today populations have grown to such an extent that there is too much sewage (which now includes industrial wastes) for simple dilution to be effective, and special treatment plants have to be used.

In the next sections, examples are given of what has happened in the past as a result of not providing clean, unpolluted and germ-free drinking water and/or an efficient sewage treatment system.

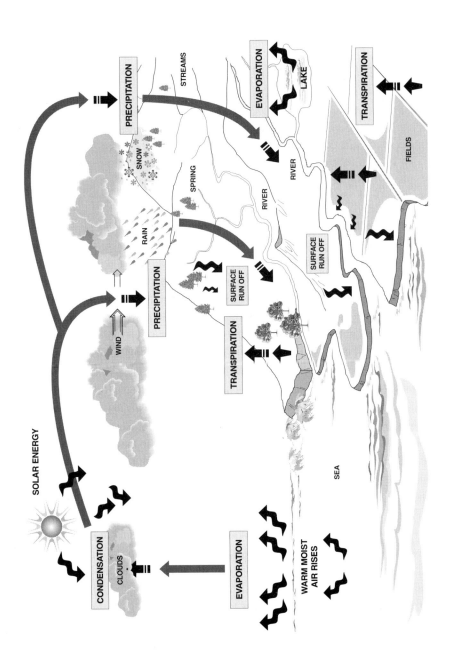

Figure 6.1

A Village called Heptonstall Slack

In the nineteenth century, a medical practitioner called Robert Howard described in great detail the sanitary condition of Heptonstall Slack, a village just north of Hebden Bridge in West Yorkshire, England. In the winter of 1843 to 1844 there had been a typhus epidemic (See Fact File 6.1) and Howard's description clearly makes the link between this disease with both the water supply and toilet facilities. Concerning the drinking water supply he describes one water spring thus,

> "...At its origin this is capital water, but along its passage it becomes, to a certain extent, loaded with vegetable matter, and during the summer and autumn, is converted into a nursery of loathsome animal life, which, aided by solar heat, is highly injurious to its quality. From the commencement to the termination of its track.... it is open and exposed, and runs over a bed of mud and slime; and the crystal stream is further polluted by the offal of a slaughter house; thus, that which is essential to the health and comfort is converted into an agent of disease".

He then turns his attention to another supply of water,

> ".. in the 'pump house', opposite the Smithy,......this water appears to hold in solution carbonate and sulphate of lime, with traces of iron; and besides containing these saline ingredients, its abominable contiguity with a privy - the partition between the well and it being merely the wall which conjoins the two buildings -"

> "... scarcely a doubt can be entrained that, in some modified form, a portion of human excrement will filter into the well, and some deleterious gas or gases float in the cavity of the well unoccupied by the water....Therefore until the privy is razed to the ground, the water can scarcely be deemed acceptable for human uses..... ".

Howard's description of the sewers and privies leaves the modern reader very thankful for the flush toilet and the sewage works. In one case he states that one stream of water

> "..discharges itself into a sewer; it is an open one; and previous to reaching the cottages..., runs through the cess pool of a privy, driving before it the agglomeration of human excrement. On its arrival at the cottages, it meets another open sewer.....They now unite in front of these habitations, and the commingled filth and detritus then pass through a sewer under one of the dwellings - the flags of the floor being its only covering - and the effluvia which permeates the seams is occasionally suffocative to the inmates. The refuse now makes its exit behind the house, and reaccumulates in a hole prepared for its reception."

In the cottages alluded to there were seven cases of fever which resulted in one death. In a second example, Howard points out the existence of a covered sewer whose opening was in the porch of a farmhouse.

> "It had no proper outlet at its termination in the field behind the house, the field being considerably above the level of the sewer, and not having been opened for twenty years, the stench emitted from its large aperture in the porch was extremely noisome....The sewer was opened, and the exhalations from it well-nigh overwhelmed the bystanders: it acted, physically, as a powerful depressant, producing nausea, vertigo, and sickness."

Six people who lived in this house contracted typhus, three subsequently dying of the disease. In the third example, Howard draws his reader's attention to

> ".....the well formerly supplied with a pump, situated in a front unoccupied room, in the centre of two hovels...The successive inhabitants of these abodes, for the space of thirty years, have made the well the reservoir of all manner of refuse. The augmenting mass of material, in its dark and loathsome location, by chemical decomposition....., became converted into offensive and putrid matter, and having, in the course of years, attained a more concentrated power, the constitution of the atmosphere in its vicinity was deeply contaminated, which, assisted by the summer and autumnal heat, rendered the inmates the victims of typhus."

Although the well was covered with a stone trough, it had a hole in it through which the matter had found its way. Howard reports a number of fever victims from these hovels, together with a few fatalities. The privies used by the villagers were crude in the extreme. The walls were made of rough, unmortared, stone and most were without a roof. None were fitted with a door and the seat was a simple pole set into the stones on either side about two feet above the ground in front of the cess pool.

London and the Year of the Big Stink

You might perhaps expect problems with water supplies and sewage in an obscure village somewhere in the north of England in the middle of the nineteenth century. The nation's capital city was also badly affected by the same problems.

In 1750, London's population was around 750 000 and the River Thames was teeming with fish. The river had always been used to dump sewage but there had not been enough to seriously pollute it. By 1840 the population had risen to over two million and sewage, together with industrial wastes, exceeded the river's natural ability to clean itself. Only eels were able to survive in its murky waters. In 1858, referred to as the Year of the Big Stink, the business of government had to be adjourned in the Houses of Parliament adjacent to the River Thames. This was because of the extremely unpleasant smell coming from the river, caused by the combination of a long, hot summer and the reduced flow of river water together with high rates of sewage discharge into the Thames. In addition, there had been three major epidemics of cholera (cf. Fact File 6.2) in London (1831-2, 1848-9 and 1853-4). Eventually after more cholera outbreaks and the continuing smell problem, a Royal Commission was set up in 1881 to try to find solutions to these problems. A major result of this Commission's work was the opening of London's first sewage treatment plant in 1889. By 1900, the population of London was over six million but six of the less sensitive fish species had returned to the river. Between World War I and World War II, London's population rose to about eight million and industry greatly increased. The sewage works were unable to cope with the demand, and by 1945 there were again no fish to be found in the Thames. In the 1950's new efforts were made to clean up the river and new sewage works were built. By 1970 fish of many kinds had returned to the River Thames.

SEWAGE TREATMENT

From the above accounts it is clear that the original object for treating sewage was to ensure that water bodies were not polluted enough to cause disease, the death of aquatic organisms or unpleasant smells. What then are the pollutants found in water and how is sewage treated?

Water pollution is the contamination of water by foreign matter such as micro-organisms, chemicals, industrial or other wastes, as well as sewage, in amounts likely to cause harm to living organisms (cf. Table 6.1). "Unclean" water can also chemically and physically damage industrial plant and equipment. Pollution causes deterioration in the quality of the water, and renders it unfit for its chosen use.

Natural waterways normally contain bacteria which enable them to undergo a process of self-purification. Indeed, the discharge of domestic sewage in small quantities to rivers can be beneficial in acting as a source of organic materials. If, however, too much is added then it can overload this self-purification process. It can lead to dissolved oxygen being used up to the extent that no animal or plant life can live in the water and a foul, extremely offensive smell will be produced. In the UK, any industrial wastes that find their way into watercourses tend not to be toxic, but if they are organic in nature and in large enough quantities they can again lead to oxygen depletion. In addition to their self-cleansing ability, because rivers are moving bodies of water, the pollution can be flushed out into the sea. Lakes, though, are particularly vulnerable to pollution because of their enclosed nature. The pollution will stay in a lake for a long time because there is no flushing out effect and the volume of water is too small to cause an effective dilution of the problem. Lakes are prone to *eutrophication*, i.e. nutrients contained in the discharges and run-offs to lakes build up and encourage the excessive growth of algae. When the algae die, their subsequent decomposition uses up dissolved oxygen to the detriment of other living things. In the case of estuaries, there are many factors that can affect the probability and the extent of pollution. These include dissolved oxygen, nutrients, indigenous

Table 6.1 Types of Water pollutants and their Effects

POLLUTANT	MAJOR SOURCES	GENERAL EFFECT	EFFECT ON THE BIOTA	EFFECT ON WATER SUPPLIES
Nitrates, phosphates and other plant nutrients.	Fertilisers, farmyard effluents, tanneries, detergents.	Causes excessive plant growth.	BOD increase.	Will need extra treatment.
Suspended solids.	Quarrying, soil erosion caused by man, pulp mills, road run-off.	Reduces amount of light entering water body. Discolours water. Coats bottom after settling.	Reduces plant's ability to photosynthesise. Blocks gills of fishes and other animals. Covers plants and animals that are bottom dwellers.	Blocks filtering systems at water treatment plants.
Surfactants.	Detergents and oils.	If forms a layer on the surface of the water can prevent carbon dioxide and oxygen interchange. Changes surface tension of the water.	Reduces the amount of dissolved oxygen. Changes in surface tension can affect the life cycle of insects.	May need extra treatment if, for example, stable foams result.
Inorganic chemicals such as acids, alkalis and salts.	Battery manufacturing. Steel, chemical and textile industries. Coal and salt mining.	The lowering or raising of acidity levels (pH).	Only a small change in pH can be tolerated by most living organisms.	Corrosion of equipment and pipes. Silting.
Toxic Chemicals.	Oil refineries and chemical companies Tanneries and wool treatment sites. Detergents. Pesticides.	Poisons living organisms.	Poisons living organisms.	Water cannot be used until levels of toxic materials are at an acceptable level. May require extensive extra treatment.
Biodegradable waste.	Domestic sewage. Food processing companies. Animal wastes.	BOD goes up. Provides food for organisms which are low down in the food chain.	Can be very serious if the BOD increases too much.	Will need extra treatment.
Pathogenic bacteria and viruses.	Raw sewage.	Bacteria can cause diseases. Action of viruses uncertain.	Can prove fatal.	Will need extra treatment.

plant and animal life, salinity, waves, tides, currents, sediments and mud. The pollution here is caused mainly by the direct input of both domestic sewage and industrial wastes, and other materials brought to the estuary by the rivers and by the tides of the sea itself.

Though sources of water pollution are large in number, they can be placed in a relatively small number of groups. These are described in Fact File 6.3.

The Nature of Sewage

When waste matter enters water, the resulting mixture is called sewage or waste water. The origin, quantity and composition of this waste are related to a society's existing life patterns. Waste water originates mainly from domestic, industrial, groundwater, and meteorological sources. These forms of waste are commonly referred to as domestic sewage, industrial waste, infiltration and storm-water drainage respectively.

Domestic sewage results from people's day-to-day activities, such as bathing, going to the toilet, food preparation and recreation. On the other hand, the quantity and character of industrial wastewater are highly varied, and depend upon the type of industry, the management of its water usage, and the degree of treatment before the wastewater is discharged. Infiltration occurs when sewers are placed below the water table or when rainfall leads to percolation down to the depth of the pipe. It is undesirable and should not occur because it imposes a greater load on the sewers and treatment plant. The amount of storm-water drainage to be carried away depends on the amount of rainfall as well as on the run-off or yield of the watershed.

The composition of industrial waste cannot be readily characterised because its composition depends on the type of manufacturing processes which have contributed to that waste. The composition of infiltration depends on the nature of the groundwater that seeps into the sewers. Storm-water sewage can contain significant concentrations of bacteria, trace elements, oil and organic chemicals.

The composition of waste water is characterised by several physical, chemical and biological measurements. The most common analyses include the measurements of amount of solids, the biochemical oxygen demand (BOD), the chemical oxygen demand (COD) and pH (See Fact File 6.4). The functions of sewage treatment are:
- to reduce the total biodegradable material, including suspended solids to acceptable levels as measured by BOD;
- to remove toxic materials;
- to eliminate pathogenic bacteria.

Sewage Treatment

There are three basic processes involved in the treatment of sewage. The first is the removal of waste matter from the sewage in the form of solid lumps or slurries of solids in water (sludges). The second is the removal of waste matter from sewage and the separated sludges by the use of micro-organisms to break down that waste biochemically. The third process is the reduction in volume of the sludges by the removal of water so that their disposal is made easier. Further details of how these stages are achieved are given in Fact File 6.5.

Since bacteria are used in the biochemical processes, if the sewage is heavily polluted with toxic substances the bacteria may be killed and the treatment will be incomplete. This would be soon detected at the sewage works and dealt with, but it can cause a lot of extra problems.

Though the ultimate disposal of the treated liquid stream is often done by direct discharge into a river, lake or the sea, in some parts of the world, waste water is re-used for a variety of purposes, e.g. groundwater recharge, irrigation of non-edible crops, industrial processes, recreation, etc. The main problem is, however, the disposal of the solid sludge waste and this is the most expensive part of the entire waste water treatment.

The final solid material is disposed of in a number of ways. The first is by land dumping where it is spread on agricultural land to condition it, and ploughed in after further drying has occurred (it is not really useful as a fertiliser because of its low nitrogen, phosphorus and potassium content). It is also dumped in ground depressions called sludge lagoons which can cause unpleasant smells, and in trenches where it is covered with soil. Other forms of getting rid of the sludge on land are by dumping it in selected refuse tips, or by mixing it with household refuse and composting it to produce organic manure. The second method involves dumping at sea. The solid waste is carried well out to sea by purpose built vessels. The problem with this is that what happens to the dumped sludge or its effects on the biota are not fully understood. The third method involves incineration. This process reduces the volume of the solid waste, destroys toxic organic compounds but leaves toxic inorganic materials in the ash.

It is clear that the process of treating sewage is complicated and involves many possible points of interaction with the environment where pollution can occur.

OUR DRINKING WATER SUPPLY

The Characteristics of Natural Water

All of the water we use has been a part of the natural water cycle at some time (cf. Figure 6.1). This cycle is based on the continuous movement of water between the surface of the Earth and the atmosphere. The part of the water cycle which provides us with our stores of fresh water involves a dynamic balance between the two processes of *evaporation* and *precipitation*. Water is evaporated from both water and land surfaces, and is *transpired* from living plant cells. The water *vapour* produced is circulated throughout the atmosphere where it is eventually precipitated as snow and rain. Snow and rain are the thus the ultimate sources of all our drinkable (potable) water - a fact that might make you feel better on a miserable, wet, rainy day.

Water has the ability to dissolve a wide range of materials so that even in its natural state (streams, rivers, lakes, *aquifers*) it is never pure. It always therefore contains a variety of dissolved *inorganic* and *organic* compounds. Water also carries large amounts of insoluble materials which are held in suspension. Both the amounts and types of impurities found in natural water vary from place to place and time of year. These natural impurities determine the characteristics of a water course (see Fact File 6.6).

Our drinking water is normally collected either from underground sources or by exploiting surface water. Underground water today is accessed by drilling and pumping. The old village well and bucket is an example of the extraction of water by digging down until the water-table is reached. Deep lying water which is under pressure can be tapped by the bore hole of an artesian well. There are three ways of obtaining surface water, pumping from rivers and lakes, building a barrage across a river and diverting its flow through a canal system, or building a dam across a valley at the lower end of a natural catchment area.

The long term storage of this collected water is via large, open reservoirs or in man made lakes.

Water Purification

The drinking water supply in most developed countries is purified by the four principal processes, viz. sedimentation, filtration, aeration and sterilisation (cf. Figure 6.2). Sedimentation is allowing water to stand in large, shallow basins or the equivalent, where solid particles sink slowly under the influence of gravity. The resulting sludge is transferred to a sludge lagoon where further settling takes place and the clear water formed recycled. Sedimentation can be helped by adding a chemical called a flocculant, e.g. *alum*, which causes small particles to clump together. If necessary, a *water softener (lime)* is added as well as *activated carbon* to

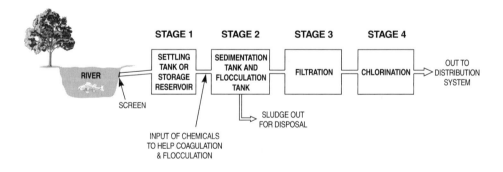

Figure 6.2 Water Purification

remove unpleasant smells, tastes or colour. Once sedimentation has occurred, the water is filtered by passing it through sand beds in which harmless bacteria decomposes any organic matter to form unobjectionable inorganic compounds. After filtration, the water is aerated by passing it over a cascade. This increases the amount of dissolved oxygen in the water and reduces the amount of dissolved carbon dioxide, thus aiding natural purification of inorganic material by aerobic bacteria. The last process involves chlorinating or adding ozone to the water in order to sterilise it, and then adding sulphur dioxide to remove the chlorine once it has done its job of killing off harmful pathogens. The water is by this stage fit for drinking.

Is our drinking water as safe as we think? In the developed countries safe drinking water is taken for granted. However, there are still many ways that water can become infected by, for example, the typhoid bacterium. In such a densely populated country as England, no stream, pond or lake is permanently safe from contamination by human excreta and therefore from contamination by this bacterium. Water supplies may be contaminated by seepage of sewage into a reservoir or surface contamination of a shallow well, leakage from defective sewers underground, discharges of sewage into a river or other water body. The bacteria can live for about a week in sewage and for longer periods of time in sewage diluted by water. So even in England we must be continuously on our guard and continue to sterilise our drinking water. In many third world countries, where the sterilisation (chlorination) of water is not carried out, there is a high child mortality rate as a consequence of disease.

The chlorination of water is not without its problems. It has caused the formation of traces of chlorinated organic compounds and there appears to be an indication that these are linked with cancer of the bladder. The current view though is that there is far greater danger from drinking untreated water than from the slight risk of bladder cancer. In many parts of Great Britain, *sodium fluoride* (optimal concentration $1\mu g$ cm^3) has been added to the drinking water to improve dental health, especially to reduce the number of fillings. This has met with opposition from a number of people who see it as a dangerous practice and one tantamount to pollution. It should be remembered that many potable waters have a natural load of fluorine in them. If you are a tea drinker then you might like to know that tea leaves are a relatively rich source of fluorine! People who live in areas where local waters supplies have a naturally high concentrations of fluorine do tend to have mottled teeth (concentrations greater than 1.5 mg a litre). It is also known that excessive intakes of fluorine (greater than 3-6 mg per litre) can cause deformed limbs (skeletal fluorosis) which can become crippling at higher concentrations (greater than 10 mg per litre).

Our water supply and the way we treat our sewage are both vital to the maintenance of good public health. Both produce waste and are involved in the treatment of waste water on a very large scale. For example, in England and Wales alone some 23×10^6 m^3 of domestic waste water and 14.1×10^6 m^3 of industrial waste water are discharged to the sewers every day. This sewage is treated by some 5000 sewage works serving about forty-four million people. As well as this, largely untreated sewage produced by a further six million people living in coastal areas is dumped in the sea and about two million people are using their own septic tank system. Very often natural water is not a threat to man, but as seen in Chapter 1, the pollution of waterways can lead to very serious consequences and must be prevented. There is no doubt that major sources of river pollution have their beginnings in the daily life of a community and in industrial operations within the water catchment area. Thus the monitoring, identification of pollutants and the subsequent treatment of water must be ensured. The next chapter deals with how we can manage water-borne wastes.

FACT FILE 6.1
Typhus

Typhus and Typhoid are two different diseases though the latter was long confused with the former. It was probably typhoid fever that Howard was referring to in the year of 1843. Typhoid fever has been one of mankind's greatest scourges. Before 1875 the disease was widespread in Britain, but the Public Health Act of that year ensured improvements in sanitation and water supplies which led to a dramatic fall in the prevalence of the disease. The disease is still a major problem in tropical and subtropical countries, and in many parts of Southern and Eastern Europe. Typhoid is derived ultimately from the faeces of a case of the disease or from a chronic carrier of the bacterium *Salmonella typhii*. Related bacteria cause an almost identical disease, paratyphoid fever. Typhoid is usually spread by the contamination of drinking water with sewage, or by flies carrying the bacteria from infected faeces to food. It can also be transmitted by typhoid carriers who handle food. For example, in 1937 in Croydon, England, there was an outbreak of typhoid caused by a carrier who excreted the bacteria in his urine. He worked in the town's wells and the urine- contaminated water supply caused an explosive outbreak causing 310 cases and 43 deaths.

Once a person has contacted the disease, the bacteria pass through the wall of the bowel and spread to the lymphatic glands, where they multiply. During this period the victim shows no symptoms - this is the incubation period of the disease. After about ten days the bacteria begin to enter the blood stream from the lymphatic glands. The victim now starts to feel ill, with headaches and various muscular aches and pains. A fever develops which rises in a regular fashion until it reaches its peak after about a week. The abdomen is uncomfortable and tender, and there is usually constipation. A faint rash may appear. In the second week of illness, the victim's condition rapidly deteriorates. Constipation gives way to diarrhoea. Mental confusion appears and the victim becomes apathetic with pinched looking face, flushed cheeks and dilated pupils. The illness reaches its peak in the third week. The victim may now progressively deteriorate and die. This classical progress of the disease is now rarely seen in the developed countries because appropriate treatment with drugs cuts short the illness.

FACT FILE 6.2.
Cholera

Cholera has been known in north-east India for centuries and still breaks out regularly. In the nineteenth century because of increased international travel, cholera spread throughout the world causing millions of deaths. During the first half of the twentieth century, the disease was confined to Asia, but since 1961 a new pandemic has spread from Indonesia to much of the rest of Asia, Africa, the Mediterranean and the Gulf Coast of North America. A few cases occur each year in Britain but mainly as a result of travellers returning from Asia or Africa. Cholera is caused by a comma shaped, mobile bacterium called a vibrio. In particular it is the bacterium *Vibrio cholerae* which causes this serious and often fatal disease in man. The main source of infection is water contaminated by human faeces containing the bacteria. This disease was once endemic in England but has now disappeared because of effective sanitation and treatment of water. Poor water hygiene is a particular contributor to the spread of the disease. Symptomless carriers of the disease are of even greater importance than the actual cases of cholera themselves in the spreading of this disease.

The main feature of the disease is severe diarrhoea due to the irritation of the bowel by the toxin produced by the bacteria. The diarrhoea is so profuse and liquid that it is given the name of "rice-water". These stools have to be collected so that the amount of fluid lost by the victim can be measured before they are disposed of in a sanitary fashion. Loss of water with contained mineral salts is the main cause of death. Protection against cholera can to a certain extent be achieved by vaccination, but the main method of prevention is in the use of proper sanitation to dispose of human excreta, supported by public health measures and health education.

FACT FILE 6.3
Sources of Water Pollution

- Discharges from water and sewage company works. These always contain organic waste and can contain industrial waste. There is also the problem of the disposal of waste containing *aluminium* residues from water treatment works.
- The washing of equipment and plant in the food and drink industries. Such washings give large but dilute volumes of effluents which contain natural organic compounds such as carbohydrates, proteins and fats. These compounds are often present in large enough concentrations to cause adverse depletion in the amount of dissolved oxygen present in water.
- A third source of water pollution is industrial wastes which contain organic effluents. The paper, wool and leather industries all use animal and plant materials and hence produce waste that contains proteins, fats, oils and putrescible solids. They also produce chemicals such as *lime*, *potash* and *chromium salts*. Pollution by *sulphides* from the leather industry can also cause considerable problems.
- Effluents containing cyanides and metals from the electroplating industry. These effluents contain a very small amount of biodegradable material.
- Discharges from the petrochemical, oil refining and pharmaceutical industries. These produce perhaps the most diverse and difficult effluents to treat.
- Seepages from industrial and domestic waste stored in landfill sites. These, as seen in Chapter 1, can contain a wide variety of chemicals which can make the problem difficult to treat.
- Run-off from land, agricultural wastes and fertilisers. If animals are allowed to range freely and farms are small and isolated, pollution by agriculture is not usually a problem. Intensive farming can cause a serious build-up of concentrated wastes. Hence this will cause problems similar to those caused by domestic sewage. The excessive use of fertilisers has caused land run-off to contaminate rivers with excessive quantities of nitrates (c.f. Chapter 7).
- Discharges from the petroleum industry which include oil spills from ships in general, oil super-tanker disasters, offshore drilling operations and the occasional war.
- Acid rain. This is caused by the combination of sulphur dioxide and the oxides of nitrogen with water in the atmosphere. The sources of such pollution and an account of its consequences are given in a later chapter.
- Radioactive materials present in the wastes from uranium and thorium mining and refining, from nuclear power plants, and from the industrial, medical and scientific use of radioactive materials.

Table 6.1 lists some types of anthropogenic pollutants and their main sources, what their general effects are on the natural characteristics of a river, and how they effect the biota and water supplies. It is clear from this table that domestic, industrial and agricultural effluents cause a variety of effects on the natural characteristics of water resources into which they are discharged. Organic pollutants can cause eutrophication and remove dissolved oxygen necessary to sustain life from the water. Toxic chemicals have an insidious effect at all levels of the food chain. Pathogens carried by water spread disease. Effluents can also change the physical properties of water. The measurement and control of water quality are therefore of crucial importance in the interests of public health and in maintaining the quality of the environment.

FACT FILE 6.4

Solid Wastes include dissolved and suspended solids. Dissolved solids are classified as those materials which will pass through a filter paper, whilst suspended solids are those that will not. Suspended solids are divided into those that will or will not settle, and is measured in terms of how many mg of the solids will settle out of one litre of waste water in one hour. All of these solids can be sub-divided into volatile or non-volatile solids, the volatile solids generally being organic material and the other solids being inorganic or mineral matter.

The BOD & PV Tests

One of the most important measures of overall water quality is the amount of dissolved oxygen that it contains. As indicated earlier, removal of oxygen is caused in the main by the biodegradation of organic matter. It is possible to measure the ultimate oxygen demand by determining the difference between the amount of oxygen dissolved in a sample of water and the amount of oxygen left after the effluent has used up as much as it can. The main problem with this is that it is very difficult to know how long to leave the sample to ensure that no further oxygen will be used up. Hence, two main tests have been devised. The first one is the BIOLOGICAL OXYGEN DEMAND (BOD) test which standardised on a five day period of biodegradation. A second test is based on the PERMANGANATE VALUE (PV) which has been standardised at periods of 3 minutes and 4 hours.

In the BOD test, the oxygen required by micro-organisms is measured as an effluent sample biodegrades. The sample is incubated at 20C in a sealed bottle for 5 days. Both the initial and final oxygen content are determined. This test has been used for well over 70 years and is still the most important indicator of organic pollution. The BOD value is a standard by which an effluent is deemed satisfactory for discharge, and is vital to the operation and design of waste treatment plants. The test relies on biological action and is a simulation of actual processes which occur in polluted watercourses or an aerobic treatment plant. It has been universally adopted as a trustworthy indication of organic pollution. However, the test is slow and therefore not suitable for rapid process control in a waste treatment plant. In addition it is not a good indicator of industrial pollutants since such wastes are toxic and often inhibit the micro-organism activity on which the BOD test relies. It is more sensitive, though, than the PV test for detecting and measuring biodegradable organic wastes.

The PV Test

This test uses a known concentration of acidified potassium permanganate to oxidise any organic and inorganic materials that are capable of being oxidised. Here the concentration of the permanganate solution is measured at the start of the test and then again after 3 minutes and 4 hours at 27C. The difference reflects the uptake of oxygen and is expressed in gm^{-3}. It has been found that the ratio of the concentration of oxygen uptake after 4 hours to that used in 3 minutes gives an indication of the origin of polluting materials and is an approximate measure of the ratio of organic to inorganic oxidisable materials.

The Chemical Oxygen Demand Test (COD)

In this test, the effluent is boiled for two hours in a mixture of potassium dichromate and concentrated sulphuric acid in the presence of a silver catalyst. This ensures the complete oxidation of most of the organic and inorganic materials present. It usually gives a higher value for the oxygen uptake than either the PV or BOD tests. Charges are levelled in the UK on industrial wastes received and treated by Water Authorities on the basis of the COD values of the wastes after the suspended solids have been allowed to settle.

The pH analysis is a measure of the acidity of a waste water sample. The more acidic it is the more corrosive is the waste water.

FACT FILE 6.5
The Sewage Treatment Plant

Raw sewage enters the sewage works, where it undergoes a preliminary screening process. The sewage is first screened using a steel mesh of some kind to remove large solid objects such as wood and rags. This ensures that the machinery is not damaged or pipelines blocked. The screened sewage is pumped to settling tanks, where grit and sand settle out under the influence of gravity. These are then removed, washed and used as filling material in, for example, road construction. The grit-free sewage is now pumped to the primary sedimentation tanks. Here some 50% of the suspended solids settle out to form sludges and the Biological Oxidation Demand (BOD) is reduced by half. In the secondary treatment stage, the sludge is pumped to the primary digestion tanks and the liquid sewage pumped to aerators. Here the liquid is mixed with bacteria-enriched activated sludge. As the sewage is aerated the bacteria oxidise the organic matter into harmless products. The aerated sewage is pumped to a final secondary sedimentation tank. At this stage the activated sludge settles out, leaving a clear effluent. The upper liquid part is filtered, treated with chlorine and then discharged into a river or the sea. The activated sludge is removed and re-used in the aerator with incoming settled sewage. Meanwhile, the sludge in the primary digestion tanks is heated in the absence of air/oxygen and kept at a temperature of 30C. The temperature speeds up the action of anaerobic bacteria which digest the sludge rapidly, producing gas and a relatively inoffensive sludge. This sludge is then pumped to the secondary digestion tanks where the digestion is completed without heating. This produces a nitrogen rich sludge and relatively pure but bacteria rich water. The sludge is then removed and after drying is used as a fertiliser or dumped. The water is drawn off and discharged into a lake, river or the sea.

FACT FILE 6.6
Natural Water and it's Composition

When rain falls, the water can follow two paths. If it is heavy rain a great deal of water will run off into streams and rivers, and eventually find its way into lakes and the oceans. The extent of this will depend upon the porosity, permeability, thickness and previous moisture content of the soil. Some of the water will remain in the soil and will be returned to the atmosphere by evaporation and moved upward by the roots of vegetation to be transpired from leaves. However, some water may manage to move downwards, under the influence of gravity, through porous rock strata until it reaches an impenetrable layer. Here it collects and becomes what is known as groundwater. Groundwater is the source of wells and of the springs that feed streams, rivers and lakes. The surface of this groundwater is called the water table. Under natural conditions, the water table will fall or rise according to prevailing weather conditions, and whether or not it is being used as a water supply to a spring or as a reservoir for human use.

During their condensation and precipitation, rain or snow dissolve carbon dioxide and any other chemicals that might be present in the atmosphere. How much is dissolved will depend on the relative solubilities of the chemicals, the temperature of the atmosphere and other factors.

In its movement on and through the surface of the earth, water will dissolve and react with minerals found in the soil and rocks. The principal dissolved chemicals derived from these minerals in both groundwater and surface water are the *chlorides, hydrogen-carbonates,* and *sulphates* of *sodium* and *potassium* together with the *hydroxides* of *calcium* and *magnesium*. Almost all natural supplies of water also contain *fluorides* to a greater or lesser extent.

Sea-water contains many soluble compounds as well as a high concentration of sodium chloride. This is because many "contaminated" streams and rivers are constantly feeding the oceans. At the same time, pure water is being constantly lost from the surface of these vast water bodies by the process of evaporation. Thus less volatile materials are left behind in ever increasing amounts and cause the saline nature of the seas and oceans to increase.

A good indication of a "safe" natural water is its ability to support complex albeit fragile ecosystems. This ability to sustain aquatic life depends on a variety of physical, chemical and biological conditions. *Biodegradable* nutrients and dissolved oxygen must be available for the metabolic activities of the *algae, fungi, protozoa* and *bacteria* which are at the bottom of the *food chain*. In addition, plant and animal growth cannot occur outside narrow ranges of temperature and pH. Suspended particles can restrict the necessary light penetration for *photosynthesis. Stratification,* both thermal and saline, can hinder the transport of necessary nutrients. Dissolved carbon dioxide, hydrogen-carbonates, carbonates, nitrates, phosphates and salts that cause hardness must all be present in the right amounts for successful functioning of the life forms in a natural watercourse. Any variation of the kinds and amounts of materials found in natural waters can have a serious adverse effect on the its biota, and on humans whose drinking water might be derived from that water.

Further Reading Chapter 6

J.E.Andrews et al, *An Introduction to Environmental Chemistry*, Oxford, Blackwell Scientific, 1996

R.H.C.Emmerson et al, *The Life Cycle Analysis of Small-Scale Sewage Treatment Processes*, Water & Environmental Management; Journal of the Institute of Water & Environmental Management, 1995, **9**, No.3

N.F.Gray, *Water Technology; An Introduction for Environmental Scientists & Engineers*, Chichester, J. Wiley, 1997

M.Hammer, *Water & Wastewater Technology* (3rd Ed.), Prentice Hall, 1995

R.Howard, *A History of the Typhus of Heptonstall Slack which prevailed during the winter of 1843-1844*, Document in possession of the author.

J.F.Tapp et al (Eds), *Toxic Impact of Wastes on the Aquatic Environment*, Cambridge, Royal Society of Chemistry, 1996

E.Zwingle, *Ogallala Aquifer; Wellspring of the High Plains*, National Geographic, 1993, **183**, No.3

CHAPTER 7

THE MANAGEMENT OF WATER AND WATER-BORNE WASTES
two types of pollution: cambridge, UK and tillamook bay, USA

In this chapter the differences between point source and diffuse pollution are explained using further examples of water pollution. The chapter also describes how the control of discharges to water and water quality is ensured by good management practices, regulated by international and national law. Problems caused by the pollution of the seas and beaches are examined. Some ways in which you can help to prevent water pollution and manage water supplies are also suggested.

CAMBRIDGE, UK, AND TILLAMOOK BAY, USA

The Cambridge Water Company is a private enterprise that supplies water to the City of Cambridge, UK, and the surrounding area. In 1976 the company bought a borehole which enabled it to deliver about 12% of the total water demands of some 250 000 people. In the middle of the 1980's, the company discovered that an organic compound called *tetrachloroethene* was present in the water. According to the 1980 EC Directive concerning the quality of drinking water, the amount of this organic material present was at an unacceptably high level. The company therefore had to stop extracting the water and to look for the source of contamination. It was found that the source was a tanning company which was using the tetrachloroethene as a solvent for degreasing animal skins. As a result of either leakage or accidental spillage, the organic liquid had found its way into the groundwater being accessed by the borehole.

Tillamook Bay, Oregon, USA, is surrounded by a thriving dairy cow industry. In its vicinity, there are approximately 25 000 dairy cattle, which not only produce milk for dairy products but also some 300 000 gallons of urine and manure a day. The average annual rainfall in the area is about ninety inches. When this heavy rain falls, usually between October and May, it causes the rivers running through the fields to flood. When this happens the oyster and clam beds in the bay are not farmed because of the fear of contamination from the cows' excrement. The dairy farmers have responded to this by building special tanks to store the manure so that it cannot contaminate the river water and hence the bay. During dry days, the manure is spread over agricultural land as fertiliser. Unfortunately, it is possible that the next wet day can reactivate the manure and cause further contamination of surface water. Problems with water resources in the USA are widespread, with 44 states reporting groundwater contaminated by run-off from farms and ranches.

What is the difference between the two examples of water pollution, and what can be done to prevent such occurrences?

Water pollution can be divided into two types: point-source pollution, as in the case of the Cambridge example, and non-point or diffuse pollution, as in the case of Tillamook Bay. Point source pollution was largely described in the previous chapter, i.e. waste water from either sewage treatment plants or from factories. In the UK, law and regulations with which producers have to comply can control the vast majority of potential, and real, point source pollution. Point source pollution is often detectable and traceable, and therefore offenders can ultimately be prosecuted. On the other hand, non-point water pollution involves what is carried by water when it eventually runs off land into various watercourses. The nature of this pollution is diverse and the pollutants numerous. An additional problem is that in the case of some aquifers it takes a long time for pollution to reach them, the damage is actually done a long time before detection and the perpetrator long gone. It is thus difficult not only to allocate blame to any one person or company, but also to trace the source(s) of such pollution. In many ways, non-point pollution is now a much more serious problem in countries like the UK than point source pollution. It is very difficult to control and apply sanctions to something or someone if you don't know where the pollution has come from or who is responsible. It is for these reasons that one could include the dumping of waste matter in our seas and oceans under the heading of non-point water pollution.

So what causes run-off to be a problem? Water is the so-called "universal solvent" in that it dissolves, to a greater or lesser extent, a wide range of materials. When it moves, the kinetic energy of the water can be such that it can carry along with it heavy objects as well as lighter suspended matter. Hence, it is easy to contaminate water either deliberately or by simply not thinking an action through. It happens when you spill oil on your driveway or pour it down the storm water drain when completing a home service on your car. It happens when a farmer treats his field of potato crop with a herbicide. It happens when you throw away an old car battery into a ditch or leave it by the side of the road. It happens when someone cleans a car part with a solvent of some kind and dumps the liquid onto the ground. It happens when a gardener treats the lawn with a fertiliser or green-up agent. It happens when you throw a spent cigarette out of your car window. When it rains, the water will pick up all types of materials - oil, solvents, nitrates, phosphates, manure, metal compounds, solid wastes, etc - and effectively concentrates them by adding to streams, rivers and lakes or to the groundwater in aquifers.

THE MANAGEMENT OF WATER POLLUTION BY REGULATION AND LAW

How can we control and thus manage water pollution and ensure the quality of our water supplies? As far as agriculture, industry and commerce are concerned the answer lies mainly in compliance with law and regulations, coupled with common sense and a respect for our environment.

In the United Kingdom, for England and Wales, the passing of the 1989 Water Act was a very important milestone. Essentially this Act did four main things. Firstly it privatised the then existing regional water authorities into ten new water and sewerage companies, e.g. Yorkshire Water. Such companies treat and dispose of sewage as well as supply water. Secondly, it established new bodies to control the water environment and to ensure that the companies operated correctly within the regulations. Thirdly, it provided for the regulation of the water companies and any other water service company appointed under the Act. Finally, it amended the law relating to water supply, sewerage, and the pollution and use of water. Because of this Act, it became an offence to knowingly permit the discharge of poisonous, noxious or polluting matter or solid waste matter into any "controlled waters", i.e. rivers, streams, lakes, ponds, canals and ditches, without proper authority.

In addition to the regional water authorities there were a number of privately owned water companies in existence that had nothing to do with sewage and its

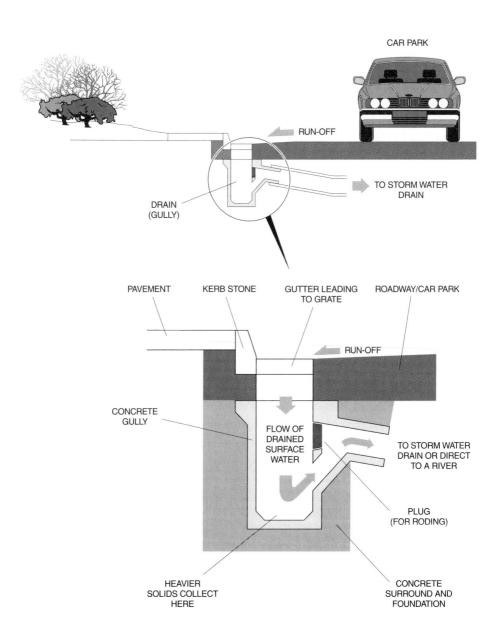

Figure 7.1 Run Off

treatment but supplied water only. There are currently eighteen such companies in operation, e.g. York Waterworks Company.

The water and sewerage service companies hope to achieve a number of aims by the correct management of natural and waste waters. With regard to "clean" water management, the first aim is the extraction from rivers, reservoirs and underground sources of the water necessary to meet demands. The second aim is to ensure that the extracted water is fit for purpose by treatment to a very high standard. The third aim is to deliver drinking water to homes and businesses. "Dirty" water management involves the collection of waste water as its first aim, followed by the treatment of that waste water to remove potential pollutants, and finally the return of the waste water safely back to the aquatic environment.

In 1991 two new acts, the Water Industry Act and the Water Resources Act, replaced the 1989 legislation. Their purpose was to consolidate all of the cumbersome legislation covering water that had previously appeared in a large number of statutes. To ensure that the aims of these Acts are carried out properly, three regulatory bodies have been established for the whole of the water industry.

The first body is the Office of Water Services (Ofwat), which is an economic regulator. The head of this organisation is someone entitled "Director General" who has the main duty of ensuring that the water companies are adequately financed to perform their functions. The Director General therefore controls the amount by which the water companies can increase their prices each year. Since privatisation, prices have been allowed to rise to increase the revenue so that money is available to fund the very large investment programmes designed to meet higher quality standards. This has been a contentious issue for some years. It can be argued that the cost of water in the UK is too low and that one way of conserving water and ensuring its high quality is by charging more. People who obtain their domestic water via a metering system pay for what they use. This includes water lost by dripping taps, taps left running, ruptured pipes, etc. One suggestion has been that your sewage rate should be linked to the number of toilets you have in your home! It has been shown, though, that metering water and charging for the amount used causes people to pay more attention to poor domestic management of their water supply. However, there are health implications in that people who are unclean in both their person and living conditions may be discouraged from using water. The resulting costs to the health service can be much higher than the extra money raised by metering water.

Ofwat also has another function, in ensuring that you, the consumer, are protected from discrimination. For example, you pay the same for your water whether you live in a well-populated urban area or a sparsely populated rural area. It is also the role of the Director General to encourage companies to be more efficient and to facilitate competition. Competition stimulates inventiveness to meet the regulations more efficiently.

The second regulatory body was the National Rivers Authority (NRA). Until 1996, all other aspects of water control in England and Wales came under the control of this body, and the Drinking Water Inspectorate and Her Majesty's Inspectorate of Pollution. In 1996, another regulatory body, the Environment Agency, was formed from the NRA, Her Majesty's Inspectorate of Pollution and the Waste Regulatory Authorities, together with some technical units from the Department of Environment. The Environment Agency now covers the management of radioactive and other forms of waste, pollution control and the management of water resources, water waste, flood defence, freshwater fisheries and conservation. The Agency thus has three key functions. The first is to protect and improve the quality of rivers, estuaries and coastal waters by effective pollution control. The second is to manage water resources, which involves balancing the needs of the environment with the needs of those who require to take water from rivers and underground sources. The third function is to protect people and property from flooding either from the sea or rivers. The Environment Agency is also responsible for fisheries, boating in some rivers and the recreational use of inland and coastal waters. (Perhaps it is worth noting at this point that boating is a source of water pollution in that human waste is normally only macerated and not treated before it goes into the water. Motor boats can also leak oil or fuel into waterways). It is through this Agency that the protection and proper management of water is carried out in England and Wales via education, prevention and enforcement.

The third body is the Drinking Water Inspectorate which regulates the quality of drinking water.

Thus it would appear that as far as England and Wales are concerned there are both laws and the bodies to apply those laws which help considerably in the management of water pollution.

CONTROLLING DISCHARGES

The large majority of point source pollution is caused by the discharge of untreated sewage or by industrial effluents otherwise known as trade waste. The most serious cases of point pollution from agricultural practices come from *slurry, silage effluents* and *dirty water* (See Fact File 7.1). These originate from one building, store or field. Trade waste originates from a wide variety of manufacturing processes such as metal mining and extraction, paper-making and food production. Indeed almost all processes produce liquid waste of some kind. The problem is that this waste is very different from sewage in that it often contains a much wider range of pollutants that are likely to be toxic. In addition, the removal of these toxic materials usually depends upon chemical and physical techniques rather than techniques involving biodegradability. Hopefully, before any industrial water-based waste leaves the premises treatment has already occurred which has rendered it harmless. Once this has been done it can be possible to combine the final treatment of the industrial effluent with that of domestic sewage, thus saving costs. The cost of disposing of trade effluent in this way, the sewage rate, is based on the strength of the effluent.

River pollution is prevented in the UK by setting legal limits on the composition of all types of effluents that are to be discharged into either surface or underground waters. Before a company can discharge an effluent, a legal document called the "consent" must first be obtained. This consent tells the discharger (i) where the discharge can take place, (ii) what the construction of the outlet will be, and (iii) what the character, chemical composition, temperature, amount (volume) together with the rate of flow of the discharge must be. Typically, the consent will cover the limits on Biological Oxidation Demand (BOD), concentrations of suspended matter, ammonia and metals present, and specify any poisonous substances that are not allowed to be present in the effluent.

During the 1950's and 1960's several Acts were passed to control discharges of effluents to inland waters, tidal waters and underground sites. In 1974, the Control of Pollution Act placed information concerning discharges and the compliance of those discharges with consent conditions in the public domain. Registers are kept so that you can see for yourself if a company or organisation is acting responsibly and legally. Indeed, it is possible for any private citizen to bring a prosecution against anyone that he or she knows is breaking consent conditions. You are now able to learn much more about local discharges and river quality in your area as a result of this Act. The fact that such knowledge is so readily available to so many interested people helps to encourage companies to be more vigilant and careful in the way they handle their waste.

Each industrial effluent is considered on its own merits when consent is being sought for its disposal in streams and rivers. Whether or not consent is given will depend upon the type of effluent, the legislation and the potential effects of that effluent on the receiving water.

Industrial effluent discharge to sewers is also strictly controlled by additional public health and other acts. Under these acts, an industrial company can discharge its effluent to the foul sewer provided that it does not adversely affect the structure of the sewers, affect anyone working in them, or damage the sewage treatment plant upon its arrival there. A consent can be imposed on a company, whether it wants one or not, and an appropriate charge made for the reception and treatment of the effluent at the sewage treatment plant.

There are extra restraints on effluents that are to be discharged underground. A company can only discharge sewage effluent to an underground site. In addition, the underground rock strata must be such that no waste can percolate any closer than 10 metres to a stream or river. Discharges must also meet the standards set down by the EC Directive on Discharges to Underground Water.

WATER QUALITY

Any effluent, and the water it is discharged into, has to be checked regularly to ensure that pollution does not occur and that no authorisation is being exceeded. Effluents from sewage sites and industrial premises are monitored at agreed sampling points both by a company's own scientists, or scientists acting on their behalf, and by scientists from the Environment Agency. These sampling points are specified in the legal consent. Environment Agency staff have free and uninhibited access to the sampling points at any time, and can either do a spot check or spend as long as they like on extensive testing. What is involved in the analysis that takes place depends on the type of effluent and on what is stated in the consent conditions. In some instances there is a charge made to the producers for this analysis.

Chemical and physical analyses typically involve the determination of BOD and Chemical Oxygen Demand (COD), pH, amounts of suspended solids, and the presence and concentrations of chloride, phosphate and nitrogen in the form of ammonium compounds, nitrites, and nitrates. How often testing is carried out will depend upon the amount of effluent that is discharged and on its potential impact on the environment.

In addition to chemical methods, the quality of water is indicated by the biological species it contains. Many different living organisms exist in normal rivers, lakes and streams. However, it must be also remembered that for a given river, the type and number of organisms is not the same at all points. There is a natural variation. These organisms differ greatly in their reaction towards changes in their environment and in their ability to resist pollutants. *Bacteria, fungi, protozoa, algae*, some plants, some *invertebrates* and fish have all been used as so-called "biological indicators" of pollution.

If a clean river becomes polluted, then the effects on the species present can be quite dramatic. There can be a reduction in the number of species present, a change in the type of species present and/or a change in the number of individuals of each species. These changes can be due to the death of the species, the movement of the organisms away from the source of pollution, or a growth in population of species that can tolerate the pollution. A living organism which inhabits the bottom of a water body and remains essentially in the same place, is particularly useful in determining the effects of pollution.

A measure of pollution at a particular site is reflected in the **biotic index**. A visual examination is made of a sample of river sediment and the species present identified. One way of determining the biotic index is using what is known as the Biological Monitoring Working Panel (BMWP) method which is in common use in the UK. It is designed to give a broad indication of the biological condition of rivers in the UK. A somewhat arbitrary score is allocated to each species according to their resistance to pollution, i.e. the more sensitive the species the higher the score and the more tolerant the species the lower the score. Only the family is identified and no account is taken of the number of family members. When all scores have been added up, the overall score gives an indication of the pollution at that site (c.f. Fact File 7.2).

Biotic indices can be used as an instantaneous measure of pollution, as a means of observing changes at a site over a long period of time, and a way of comparing different sites. One of the main advantages of using a biotic index compared with chemical methods of analysis is that living organisms continue to show the effects of intermittent pollution over a long period of time. The sample(s) is tested only at that time and at that place. Subsequent checks will normally show a variation. It is possible to sample a stream for chemical testing when the pollution is temporarily not present or when a pollution source has passed by. Organisms in a stretch of water also respond to all pollutants both known and unknown. Their response may tell an investigator that something is present in the water that they had not initially thought about.

However, care must be taken when interpreting a biotic index because pollution may not be the only thing that is affecting the organisms, e.g. how fast a river is flowing will also affect the species present.

A Water Service Company has to decide what steps it has to take to maintain and develop each stretch of river in its area. It has to give details concerning the level of the quality of water it wishes to maintain whilst taking into account the uses to which each stretch of river will be put. It has been common practice to give a blanket set of consent conditions which are not really related to the needs of the river. Indeed, the conditions imposed have often been set beyond the capabilities of the plant available for the treatment of water waste. Hence, each Water Service Company has to review its consent regularly. In the short-term, this review tries to give a realistic forecast of effluent quality which the plant can achieve under good management. In the longer term it attempts to monitor the needs of the river and its river quality objectives.

Legal action is usually taken against persistent offenders who do not comply with consent conditions. The consent system relies, to a large extent, on negotiation and mutual agreement between the regulators and the dischargers.

Drinking water standards ultimately depend upon the cleanliness of the water from which the water is extracted, so a badly polluted source can be of great danger. In 1993, run-off from farmland deposited the parasite called *Cryptosporidium* (cf. Fact File 7.2) into the drinking water source in Milwaukee, Wisconsin, USA. As a consequence of this, thousands of people became ill and about a hundred who suffered from immune-system deficiencies such as AIDS and leukaemia died. Cattle manure was amongst the suspected sources. In recent years, orders for the boiling of drinking water were issued in the Hull and Doncaster areas England, UK, because of the presence of these protozoa.

The 1989 Water Act established what constitutes appropriate quality for drinking water in England and Wales. The standards that were set matched those laid down by the EC Directive on the Quality of Drinking Water Intended for Human Consumption. What materials are allowed to be present in our drinking water, and what their maximum or minimum concentrations can be, are clearly set down. Our drinking water is described as being "wholesome" if it matches these conditions. Again, as in the case of effluent monitoring, the position and number of sampling points, the frequency of sampling for all chemical and biological parameters, and the way in which tests are carried out are all specified. If you knew that the water in the liquid you have recently drunk has probably already been passed through half a dozen or more people before it has got to you, then the importance of waste water management becomes rather obvious!

DEATH IN THE MEDITERRANNEAN SEA

Most people enjoy watching dolphins whilst others, unfortunately, like eating them! In general they are admired for their intelligence, grace, mischievousness, and apparent liking for human beings, and are popular performers in aquariums (another point for debate!). Between 1990 and 1991 several thousand dolphins died in the Mediterranean Sea (see Fact File 7.4). They were killed by a virus that caused pneumonia and brain damage, and apparently lowered their resistance to diseases. (In 1989, a similar virus killed 20000 common seals in the North Sea). The first dead animals were found on the coast of Southern Spain but the virus soon spread to the rest of the Mediterranean Sea. Dead dolphins were found on the beaches of Morocco, Algeria, France, Italy and eventually the Greek Islands of the Aegean Sea. Schools of dolphins were reduced to one-third of their size at the height of the epidemic. A number of scientists believed that industrial chemicals polluting the Mediterranean Sea had caused the demise of the dolphins. These chemicals, it is suspected, had affected the dolphin's immune system, making them susceptible to the disease. Compounds such as *polychlorinated biphenyls* (PCBs) were found in the organs of the dolphins. Such compounds are not miscible with water and therefore become concentrated in plankton. Hence, the fish that eat the plankton also concentrate the chemicals in their flesh, and ultimately in their predators, the dolphins.

The Mediterranean Sea has a coastline of about 46 000 kilometres with some 130 million people living along it. During the tourist season a further 100 million people swell these ranks. About 80% of their untreated sewage, some 500 million tonnes per year, is dumped into the sea. Consequently, many of the beaches have failed the standards of cleanliness set for them by the European Union Bathing Waters Directive. Health hazards are increased because the warm waters of the Mediterranean Sea encourage the development of *pathogens* and, because bathers stay in the water longer, the development of diseases.

In addition to the sewage, according to the United Nations Environment Programme, some 12 000 tones of mineral oils, 60 000 tonnes of detergents, 100 tonnes of mercury, 3 800 tonnes of lead, 3 600 tonnes of phosphates enter the sea each year as a result of human activity on the land. Oil tankers and other ships regularly criss-cross the sea, and some one million tonnes of crude oil per year is dumped from these ships. This is a result of the lack of collection points for waste oil in harbours or proper facilities for cleaning tanks. The Mediterranean Sea has been, and continues to be, heavily polluted by mankind - it is a sea undergoing potential ecological and species disasters that may be irreversible.

It was realised much earlier than 1992 that there was a problem. In 1975, 11 countries with an interest in the Mediterranean Sea had met to see what could be done about its polluted condition and to improve the marine environment. In 1976, 17 countries signed the Barcelona Convention, designed to lead to a clean-up and banning the dumping of mercury, cadmium, DDT, crude oil, hydrocarbons and their derivatives, and persistent plastics. Nothing was done, so that in 1985 another meeting was convened. Here it was decided that cities with a population greater than 100000 would have new sewage treatment plants, new efforts would be made to cut industrial pollution, endangered species would receive protection, and 50 new nature reserves would be established. A report in 1990 showed that 93% of the shellfish taken from the Mediterranean Sea contained more faecal bacteria than the maximum recommended by the World Health Organisation. By 1995 it was difficult to judge what was going on and being done by individual countries. Currently the major problem is *eutrophication* due to the influx of nitrates and phosphates from sewage, detergents, fertilisers and slurry from farms.

Any dissolved materials or suspended particulate matter in a river will ultimately find their way to the sea. When fresh water and salt water mix the distribution of chemicals between the two different types of water can change. The particulate matter can desorb chemicals already attached to its surfaces into the sea, or adsorb new chemicals from the sea. Chemical *precipitation* also results in the formation of new chemicals that remain suspended in the seawater or settle as sediments. Thus the chemical environment that a living organism can find itself in can be changed for the worse. In addition, fresh water is less dense than salt water and therefore will float on top of seawater, i.e. the water becomes stratified, unless there is some turbulent process going on which causes mixing. What fresh water carries depends on the catchment area and what we discharge into it, together with the results of erosion processes.

As a result of the increasing usage of land for agriculture and the increase in agricultural practices such as the extensive use of fertilisers, there has been a gradual build-up of the amount of nitrates in UK and other European rivers. These nitrates sooner or later enter the sea. Other discharges to the sea include sewage sludge, dredging spoil and raw sewage.

Associated directly with pollution of the sea is the condition of bathing beaches at sea side resorts. Long outfall pipes that go well out to sea are often used to deliver sewage away from beaches. This effluent is then diluted and broken up by the sea and the action of wind and waves. Organic matter is broken down by bacterial action very similar to that occurring in sewage treatment works. Although salt water and ultra-violet light both act as disinfectants to kill germs found in the sewage, many viruses survive.

However, it is still possible to get faecal matter on beaches and the swimming areas by the action of strong onshore winds and thermal currents in the sea. How would you feel about swimming in such contaminated water? There is some experimental evidence that shows there are more potentially hazardous bacteria to be found in bathing areas near to a long outfall pipe but there is very little evidence to suggest that these have increased diseases in humans. The answer seems to be not to take the risk in the first place, and to treat all of our human-based sewage on land.

Litter on beaches is nearly as big a problem, though less feared, as it is on the streets of our towns. Litter may be more obvious and understood than some of the "exotic" pollutants mentioned so far in this book, but it is just as polluting. Some beach litter is plainly hazardous, e.g. drums of chemicals washed overboard from ships. There are three main ways a beach becomes littered, by contamination with sewage, by visitors dropping their litter, and by materials dumped in the sea. The first two can be relatively easily managed by changing existing technology or personal practices, and by the imposition of law. Dumping at sea is far more problematical even with international and national anti-dumping laws in operation.

Heavy materials like tin cans and bottles will eventually sink to the sea-bed, paper and food related materials will rapidly biodegrade in the marine environment.

Plastics are a major problem because they are less generally dense than water and therefore float. Many are also non-biodegradable. Thus waste plastic lies around our environment for a very long time. Plastic material is particularly hazardous to wildlife in terms of ingestion (both via the digestive system and respiration system) and entanglement. In the latter case, lost plastic drift nets that "hover" in the sea have entrapped large numbers of fish and other organisms which in turn have attracted their predators to an untimely death. This has led to a ban on the use of such nets in certain countries.

In 1990 the UK was a signatory to the North Sea Conference which agreed a number of measures to help clean up the sea and reduce further pollution. It was decided that a number of toxic substances emitted into rivers and the atmosphere would be reduced by 50% by 1995. The more harmful pollutants such as mercury, lead and dioxins were to be reduced by 70% (compared with the available 1985 figures). There was to be a substantial reduction in the amount of pesticides and nutrients reaching the North Sea. PCB's were to be phased out by 1999 at the latest. As far as possible proper sewage treatment was to be available for all urban areas with

Figure 7.2 - Plastic Rubbish in a French Harbour (Photo taken by the author)

five thousand or more inhabitants or equivalent amounts of "dirty" water from industry. There was to be an improvement in the quality of dredged materials disposed of in the sea. Regulation of the amounts of manure and fertiliser in agricultural processes was to occur. Incineration at sea was to be phased out by 1991.

Since the UK is part of the European Community (EC) it complies with EC Regulations. EC directives have played a great part in bringing about changes in the control of water pollution in the UK. There are directives applicable to a whole range of water quality matters, such as the quality of drinking water, the quality of bathing beaches and individual pollutants. Thus both national and international legislation work together to ensure water quality is properly managed.

To help achieve the aims of the North Sea Conference agreement and to implement the EC directives, the UK drew up a "red list" of chemicals which are the most damaging to the environment. Control of these chemicals is covered by the Environmental Pollution Act of 1990. The Act introduced the idea of integrated pollution control where, after carefully weighing the pros and cons, polluting releases are allowed to go to that part of the environment (land, water or air) which results in the least amount of damage being done.

"WATER, WATER, EVERYWHERE: NOR ANY DROP TO DRINK"

We have seen that sewage can be a major polluting source of our waterways. If it is not treated properly it can kill living organisms in the environment, cause sickening smells, be visually offensive and cause the death of human beings. Untreated trade waste can lead to similar problems. Problems concerning waste water cannot be simply solved by the application of existing, or the passing of more, law. It is also a matter of seeing the need to place the use and protection of the environment and its resources in the forefront of company and government thinking. What is important is what is done or not done! Managers should adopt an approach which continually looks for improvement in their environmental targets and one that always searches for better ways of preventing water pollution. Certainly, any reduction in emissions to water not only reflects efficient resource management but can bring economic advantages to a company as well. One way we can prevent water pollution from potential point sources relatively easily is by making the removal of those pollutants part of an integrated waste management system.

Much water pollution occurs as a consequence of what enters our streams, rivers and aquifers from diffuse sources of pollution. We have seen in this chapter what can happen as a result of taking water for granted and assuming that even a vast body of water like the Mediterranean Sea can absorb everything that is dumped into it. All people can contribute to reducing the pollution of water by controlling what they allow to go to drains. Many of us still think of industrial companies such as oil producers and users as being the major water polluters. At a personal level, how many of us regard ourselves as potential contributors to the problem? Remember, what the rain sweeps from our streets, driveways and car parks will be carried to our waterways. Hence, we shouldn't throw away anything which can cause water pollution. Even when we are enjoying leisure activities such as boating, bathing and fishing we can still be responsible for polluting our waters. All we have to do is to appreciate the consequences of some of our actions and act a little more responsibly. There is a vast amount of water in our world! There isn't a water shortage! A lot of potable water, though, is not always in the right place at the right time, or of the right quality to drink.

FACT FILE 7.1
Agricultural Waste

According to the UK Ministry of Agriculture, Fisheries and Food (MAFF), **slurry** is produced from dairy and beef cattle or pig housing which does not have much straw or bedding material. Its appearance can range from a semi-solid with about 12% dry matter to a liquid with 3-4% dry matter. The composition depends upon how dilute the slurry is and on the type of animals producing it.

Silage is the name given to fodder that is preserved and stored by farmers to provide feed during the winter. The large, round, brick or metal containers in which it is stored are called **silos**. These can be above ground structures or simply a concrete-lined excavation in the soil. Green material is placed in the silo where it undergoes controlled fermentation. Precise amounts of air and temperature control are used to produce a very nutritious food source. Sometimes extra nutrients are added, e.g. sugars, to increase the speed of the process and to increase the nutritional value of the feed. The effluent from crops stored in a silo, or in an enclosed pit, is one of the most concentrated and harmful pollutants on a farm. Even small amounts can cause serious environmental damage if let out accidentally. It is very corrosive and can damage concrete and steel. Silage effluent cannot be treated and then discharged into a watercourse. It has to be stored safely, then spread onto land or used in animal feed.

Dirty water is closely allied to slurry. It is waste that contains less than 3% dry matter. It is made up of water contaminated by manure, urine, crop seepage, milk, other dairy products, and cleaning materials. It originates from cleaning work and run-off from open concrete areas that are often dirtied by manure or silage. Hence, it can be a lot more polluting than yard run-off or cleaning water. The BOD and the amount of plant nutrients in dirty water can vary considerably. All dirty water is a lot more polluting than raw domestic sewage. It has to be collected, stored and disposed of carefully.

To give you some idea of the potential effects on living organisms should agricultural waste find its way into the environment, the following BOD levels are quoted.

WASTE	BOD/mgl^{-1}	WASTE	BOD/mgl^{-1}
Treated domestic sewage	20-60	Cattle slurry	10 000-20 000
Raw domestic sewage	300-400	Pig slurry	20 000-30 000
Dilute dairy parlour and		Silage effluent	30 000-80 000
yard washings (dirty water)	1 000-2 000	Milk	140 000
Liquid sewage sludge	10 000-20 000		

FACT FILE 7.2
An Example of the Use of Biotic Indices

The simplified list below will give an idea of how clean a river is - a high score and the presence of sensitive organisms will be a good indicator that a river is clean.

ORGANISM TYPE	SCORE
Mayfly nymphs (e.g.Emphemeridae)	
Stonefly nymphs (all families) 10	
Damselfly and dragonfly (all families)	
Freshwater crayfish (Astacidae) 8	
Cased caddis larvae (all families)	
Caseless caddis larvae (e.g.Rhyacophilidae) 7	
Freshwater shrimp (Gammaridae)	
Freshwater limpet (Ancylidae) 6	
Water bugs & beetles (all families)	
Flatworm (all families) 5	
Alderfly larvae (Sialidae)	
Mayfly nymphs (Baetidae only) 4	
Snails (e.g. Lymnaediae)	
Leeches (all families)	
Water mites (all families) 3	
Fly larvae (Chironomidae only) 2	
True worms (all families)	
Fly larvae (e.g. Culicidea) 1	

You can see from the above table that a particular family of a species is identified in some cases, e.g. the two types of fly larvae. This is indicative of how sensitive different families are to the presence of pollution.

How is the above table used? Let us assume that a sample of water and sediment is taken from the bottom of a lake. The species found in this sample together with their respective scores are shown below:-

Mayfly nymphs from the Emphemeridae and Baetidae families . . . 10 and 4
4 types of stonefly nymphs. . . . . 10 x 4 =40
Freshwater crayfish 8
1 type of cased caddis larvae 7
Freshwater shrimps 6
3 types of snails . . . . 3 x 3 = 9
Fly larvae from the Culicidae family 1
The total score is therefore . . . . . 10 +4 + 40 + 8 + 7 + 6 + 9 + 1 = 85

Such a high score would indicate that the water was clean!

The above gives an idea of how biotic indices may be used to calculate an overall score. There are other types of biotic indices apart from the one listed here.

FACT FILE 7.3
The Trouble With Cryptosporidium

Cryptosporidium is a common parasite found in the lining of the intestinal tract of humans and animals. It is a single celled animal of the *protozoa* family, and is found throughout the world. It is spread from animals to humans, as well as from person to person by faecal-oral routes. The infection is often acquired from drinking water, and occasionally from infected swimming pools when the accidental ingestion of water has taken place. The infection, often occurring in childhood, can last up to three weeks and is characterised by watery diarrhoea and abdominal pain. In immune-deficient persons such as AIDS victims, the infection can be widely spread throughout the body, and diarrhoea is persistent (lasting for months or years) and can be life threatening. The parasite is so small that great care must be used in finding it with a microscope. The protozoon can surround itself with a membrane to become what is known as a cyst. These cysts are difficult to kill and treatment is not very effective. The organism is not fully removed by sewage treatment processes. They are small enough to pass through filters used in drinking water treatment. They are unaffected by chlorination but are killed by ozone. Their numbers can be greatly reduced by filtering through carefully operated slow sand filters. There is a clear link between this infection and the pollution of rivers by farm run-off and sewage from an infected population.

FACT FILE 7.4
The Mediterranean Sea & Dolphins

The Mediterranean Sea is an inland sea which separates Europe from North Africa, with Asia in the form of the Near East to the extreme east. Its greatest length is about 3700 kilometres and it has a maximum width of about 1600 kilometres. Its surface area is about 2966000 square kilometres. Its maximum depth is 5150 metres. The Mediterranean Sea is linked to the Atlantic Ocean through the Strait of Gibraltar, to the Red Sea and the Indian Ocean via the Suez Canal, and to the Black Sea via the Bosphorus. It is subdivided into four main seas, the Adriatic, Aegean, Ionian and Tyrrhenian seas. It is a saltier sea than the Atlantic Ocean because of the narrow tide range (it is almost tideless) and the high rate of evaporation. Its denser sea water causes a permanent deep current flow out into the Atlantic. Several large rivers (and their tributaries) flow into the Mediterranean Sea, i.e. the Nile, Po, Rhone and Ebro.

Dolphins belong to a highly intelligent family of aquatic mammals (family Delphinidae) which includes the porpoises. There are about 60 species. Most dolphins are found in temperate and tropical seas, but there are a small number of fresh water dolphins to be found in rivers in Africa, Asia and South America. Dolphins are those species which have a beak-like snout and slender body. Porpoises are smaller with a blunt snout and stocky body. The common dolphin, *Delphinus delphis*, is found in all temperate and tropical seas. It grows to a length of up to 2.5 metres and is dark above and white below with bands of yellow, white and black on the sides. Its mouth contains so many teeth which make its "beak" protrude forward from the rounded head. The corners of its mouth are permanently upturned so that it looks as if the animal is smiling. Endearing, but dolphins cannot smile! In fact, these animals have very little to smile about. These mammals feed on fish and squid. The species most often seen is the bottle-nosed dolphin, *Tursiops truncatus*, which is found in warm seas. These animals are grey in colour and grow to a maximum of about 4.2 metres. The intelligence of these animals is such that the United States navy trained Dolphins for military purposes. In 1987 six dolphins were sent to the Persian Gulf to detect mines. All dolphins are often threatened by man - they are trapped in fishing nets, killed by speedboats and poisoned by pollution. In 1990 countries bordering on the North Sea agreed to introduce law to protect dolphins.

Note. For an explanation of the names given to living organisms please see Appendix 4.

Further Reading Chapter 7

N.F.Gray, *Drinking Water Quality; Problems and Solutions*, Chichester, J.Wiley, 1994

M.K.Jermar, *Water Resources & Water Management, Oxford*, Elsevier, 1987

D.Kinnersley, *Coming Clean, London*, Penguin, 1994

M.Luker, *Control of Pollution from Highway Drainage Discharges*, London, Construction Industry Research & Information Association, 1994

C.F.Mason, *Biology of Freshwater Pollution (3rd Ed.)*, Harlow, Longman Scientific & Technical, 1996

J.F.McEdowney & S.McEdowney, *Environment and the Law: an Introduction for Environmental Scientists and Lawyers*, Harlow, Longman, 1996

Open University Course team, *Water Quality, Analysis & Management,* T237, Units 5-6 Environmental Control & Public Health, Milton Keynes, Open University Press, 1993

J. Stauffer, *The Water Crisis: Finding the Right Solutions*, London, Earthscan, 1998

CHAPTER 8

POLLUTION OF THE ATMOSPHERE
death in bhopal and london

Bhopal and London are used as examples to illustrate some of the causes and effects of point and non-point source pollution of our atmosphere. The types, sources and health effects on humans of atmospheric pollutants are described. Three major atmospheric problems, ozone depletion, the greenhouse effect and acid rain, are discussed. Some suggestions for the management of air pollution are presented.

BHOPAL AND AIR POLLUTION - THE RESULTS OF AN INDUSTRIAL ACCIDENT

Between the 2 and 3 of December 1984, the people of Bhopal, a city in central India, became only too aware of what can happen if the local atmosphere becomes polluted as a result of an industrial accident. Unfortunately, this poisoning of the atmosphere also coincided with a natural meteorological effect called a temperature inversion (cf. Fact File 8.1). Thus the consequences of the accident were far more terrible than might otherwise have been the case. So what happened at Bhopal?

The American Union Carbide Company had established a factory in the city which made pesticides for third world countries. One of the substances involved was a highly reactive chemical called *methyl isocyanate* which was stored in underground tanks. This toxic gas was accidentally leaked into the air, causing the death of at least 3 300 people and affecting over 200 000 others. Many of the affected people were blinded and suffered kidney failure. Such was the carnage that the Indian government had to call for volunteers to fly to Bhopal to help the armed forces clear the bodies of dead people and animals from the streets. For a period of time after the disaster, the skies over Bhopal were described as glowing red from the hundreds of funeral pyres. It was the worst industrial accident in history. In 1989, after four years of litigation, the US company agreed to pay the Indian Government 440 million dollars in compensation. In return, the government agreed to drop criminal charges against the company and its former chairman.

Such local accidents of a "one-off" nature very often result in obvious, immediate effects and do not pose national or international pollution problems. Industrial companies can be made immediately accountable, legal action taken and appropriate recompense extracted. The cleaning up of the environment can be more problematical but again tends to be restricted to a locality. International sympathy is often expressed and financial and technical assistance provided. However, many other emissions to the atmosphere do cause problems on an international scale. In the next sections we will identify these major atmospheric pollutants, where they come from and what their effects are that cause so much concern.

AIR POLLUTION

There have been numerous cases of human activities causing the emission of gaseous, liquid and solid wastes to our atmosphere. Indeed, it could be argued that since the industrial revolution began in England, it was here that damage to the environment and public health on a large scale first began. Atmospheric emissions continue to frequently endanger the lives of a wide variety of living things including human beings. These emissions can also attack paper and building materials, reduce visibility or produce offensive smells.

It is noteworthy that amongst air pollutants emitted by natural sources only the radioactive gas radon is recognised as a major health threat.

Each year the industrially developed countries produce billions of tons of atmospheric emissions. Although many of these pollutants come from readily identified sources, it is not so easy to be as certain about their effects on our planet. However, there have been enough large-scale global effects identified to have caused concerns to governments, scientists, pressure groups and the public. Some major emissions and their sources are summarised in Table 8.1.

Table 8.1 Major Air Pollutants

POLLUTANT	MAJOR SOURCES	HUMAN HEALTH EFFECTS
Carbon monoxide (CO)	Spark ignition combustion engine (motor vehicle exhausts). Some industrial processes.	Displaces oxygen in the blood stream. Effects depend upon concentration and exposure time. Can include reduction in mental and physical abilities, and eventually death.
Carbon dioxide (CO_2)	All combustion/burning processes.	Possibly injurious to health only at very high concentrations. If in sufficient quantities can cause tiredness and affect judgement. Asphyxiation can result. Atmospheric levels have risen from about 280 ppm a century ago to a value currently at over 350 ppm.
Sulphur dioxide (SO_2)	Heat and power generators that use the fossil fuels. Coal is the single largest source. Smelting of non-ferrous ores. Manufacture of sulphuric acid.	Short term exposure to low concentrations affects lung function. Higher concentrations cause chemical bronchitis and tracheitis (an inflammation of the trachea or windpipe), and can lead to increased mortality rate.
Nitrogen oxides or NO_x (Mainly NO and NO_2)	Motor vehicle exhausts. Heat and power generators. Nitric acid manufacture. Use of explosives. Welding processes. Fertiliser manufacturing plants.	Impaired lung function at low concentrations. Increase in number of acute respiratory illnesses. Lung tissue damage.
Lead (Pb)	Motor vehicle exhausts. Metal production. Thermal power plants and other coal combustion plants.	Children are particularly sensitive to lead poisoning. Lead has been shown to affect many of the body systems, e.g. renal, reproductive, nervous.
Particulate matter	Power plants, industrial processes, motor vehicle exhausts, domestic coal burning and industrial incinerators.	Short-term exposure causes respiratory distress, lung impairment and increased mortality.

POLLUTANT	MAJOR SOURCES	HUMAN HEALTH EFFECTS
Hydrocarbons (such as ethane, propane, ethene, butanes, pentanes, ethyne, benzene).	Motor vehicle emissions. Solvent evaporation. Industrial processes. Solid waste disposal. Combustion of fuels.	No generalisations can be made. Damage caused is chemical compound specific.
Photochemical oxidants (primarily ozone O_3; also peroxyacetyl nitrate (PAN) and aldehydes).	Formed in the atmosphere by reaction of nitrogen oxides and hydrocarbons with sunlight.	Eye, nose and throat irritation, chest discomfort, coughs and headache.

LONDON AND AIR POLLUTION – THE EFFECTS OF COAL-BURNING DOMESTIC FIRES

Between the 4 and 9 of December 1952 occurred the most infamous "pea-souper" smogs recorded in the UK. This smog caused a range of cardiovascular and respiratory disorders which ultimately resulted in 4000 deaths above what would normally be expected for that time of year. 90% of these deaths occurred in people who were 45 years old or over, and the deaths of infants below the age of one doubled. People were killed by inhaling water droplets that were at least as acidic as lemon juice. The smog was caused by a temperature inversion, which when coupled with no wind, held down a vast acidic cloud. By the 9 December, the radius of this cloud extended some 30 km from the centre of London. The acid which caused the deaths was probably sulphuric acid since the levels of sulphur dioxide in the smog proved to be very high. The incident prompted legislation to be implemented and resulted in the Clean Air Acts of 1956 and 1968. Even so, London is still not free of smogs.

Between the 13 and 15 December 1991, a severe smog was produced which showed high levels of nitrogen dioxide at ground level. The conditions arose because of a high-pressure system which brought settled weather and created warm dry air at higher altitudes. The air at ground level started to cool and cold, moist air began to rise. This was trapped below a layer of warmer air. The cold air stagnated because of the lack of wind. A density inversion was therefore created over London and the pollutants remained trapped near street level to cause a smog. Heavy traffic at the time made matters much worse. Fortunately, no adverse effects on health were reported but it resulted in the worst record of NO_X pollution since measurements began in 1976.

THE OZONE PROBLEM

Ozone is a highly toxic and irritant gas which readily breaks down to oxygen. In doing so it releases a highly reactive oxygen **atom** which can do a great deal of damage. Oxygen exists in the atmosphere at ground-level as **molecules** and is, of course, vital to animal and plant life. You may have smelt the peculiar odour of ozone whilst standing next to a photocopier. Indeed, regulations are in force in the UK which are designed to protect users of photocopiers from the effects of ozone.

One of the major concerns of recent times has been the observed depletion of the amount of ozone in the ozone layer. The ozone found in the stratosphere (cf. Fact File 8.1) is a natural shield which protects us directly from the harmful effects of some of the sun's ultra-violet rays. Ozone is also involved in the control of temperature in the stratosphere. If the amount of ozone is reduced in this part of the upper atmosphere, then it will become cooler and the troposphere will become warmer. The overall effect will be a cooling of the Earth's surface. However, the extent of this cooling will depend on where exactly you live, i.e. upon latitude, altitude and the season of the year. Since 1977, scientists have found that there has been a significant depletion in the amount of ozone found in the stratosphere. The chemicals causing this depletion have been identified as CFCs and other man-made chemicals which have been allowed to enter the atmosphere. It should, though, be remembered that some natural processes such as volcanic eruptions have also aided this depletion by producing ozone-destroying pollutants. It has also been established that stratospheric ozone has been destroyed, particularly over the Antarctic pole following the Antarctic spring, because of the very cold ice-clouds that form, which help reactions that cause the destruction of ozone. So not all ozone depletion is caused by man.

It has also been suggested that an increase in the amount of carbon dioxide in our atmosphere as a result of the burning of fossil fuels may also cause an increase in ozone depletion. The presence of too much atmospheric carbon dioxide could cause an excessive warming up of the troposphere (see next section), which may then result in an increase in the amount of cloud cover and a consequent increase in the rate of ozone destruction. However, the exact role of carbon dioxide in ozone depletion is still not fully understood.

The main cause for concern regarding ozone depletion is that any major reduction in this gas reduces its role in preventing the solar radiation, which can kill unicellular organisms and damage the surface cells of animals and plants, from reaching the Earth's surface. For example, an increase in human skin cancers has already been confirmed in countries like New Zealand and Australia, and this has been blamed on the reduction of ozone in our atmosphere. Could it be argued, though, that the increase is related to a life style which encourages the more frequent exposure of more areas of skin to the sun? Compare, for example, photographs of sunbathers in the 1950's with those of the 1990's.

As well as the problems associated with ozone depletion, there are also problems with an increase in ozone concentrations in the troposphere, particularly at ground level, in industrialised and heavily populated areas. Ozone is classified as a secondary pollutant and has been detected at quite substantial levels in the atmosphere in urban areas, particularly on sunny mornings, and is a contributor to smogs (c.f. Fact File 8.2). The production of ozone is caused by exhaust fumes from the motor car engine reacting with the oxygen normally found in the atmosphere. Ozone will cause lung damage and further irritates existing respiratory problems. If present at sufficiently high levels it can be lethal.

THE GREENHOUSE EFFECT

Another concern caused by atmospheric pollution is the apparent increase in the so-called "greenhouse effect". The Earth's atmosphere is warmed because short wavelength ultraviolet solar radiation which reaches the Earth's surface is re-radiated back into the atmosphere as longer wavelength infra-red radiation. This infra-red radiation is absorbed and re-radiated by certain gases in our atmosphere, and this causes our planet to be warmer than it would otherwise be. These gases include water vapour, carbon dioxide, methane, tropospheric ozone, nitrous oxide, ammonia, CFCs and the *halons*. Each gas exists for different periods of time in the atmosphere and has a different ability to cause global warming.

Any increase in these atmospheric gases caused by man's activities may lead to global warming. However, the situation is a very complex one. There are many effects occurring in the atmosphere which can have a negative effect on the ability of these gases to produce a greenhouse effect. It is by no means certain what the real result will be if there is an increase in the concentrations of greenhouse gases. Nevertheless, this remains a real concern.

If global warming is a reality then changes may occur in global weather patterns. For example, there could be an increase in the severity of storms and droughts, and an overall rise in sea-level of the order of 50-60 cm by the year 2100 caused by the thermal expansion of oceans and the melting of ice-caps.

Acid Rain - A Case of International Pollution

Acid rain is caused by the reactions of (i) carbon dioxide with water to form carbonic acid; (ii) sulphur dioxide with oxygen and water to form sulphuric acid, and (iii) the oxides of nitrogen with water to form nitric acid. In particular, acid rain is a serious problem in industrialised regions and countries where the combustion of fossil fuels releases large quantities of sulphur dioxide into the atmosphere. Some regions are polluted because of acidic deposition caused by industrial processes going on in other countries that are up-wind. For example, acid rain damage to Scandinavian lakes and streams appears to be mainly due to emissions from Central European power plants and motor vehicles.

It is the combustion of coal, oil and petrol which accounts for much of the airborne pollutants involved. For example, more than 80% of the sulphur dioxide, 50% of the oxides of nitrogen, and 30-40% of the particulate matter emitted to the atmosphere in the United States are produced by fossil-fuel fired electricity generating power stations, industrial boilers and domestic fires. 80% of the carbon monoxide, and 40% of the oxides of nitrogen come from the burning of petrol and diesel in cars and lorries.

What are the effects of acid rain that have given rise to much concern? In the 1980's it was discovered that very large areas of forest in Europe and the United States were showing signs of damage, particularly those forests at higher altitudes.

In Europe, for example, it was estimated that about 5% of the forests were severely damaged and 0.2% have been killed. In what was West Germany, four of the most important tree species (Norway Spruce, White Fir, Scots Pine and Beech) showed signs of damage. The perceived effects of acid rain was so dramatic that the Germans coined a new term for it "Waldsterben" or "forest death". The area affected to a greater or lesser extent was estimated to have increased from 8% in 1982 to 54% in 1986. In Eastern Europe, the problem was even more severe, with 16% of Czech forest being badly damaged. This was partly blamed on the burning of brown coal (lignite) which has a high sulphur content.

Similar damage was also being reported in other parts of the world, e.g. in the USA, the Appalachians, Adirondack Mountains, the White Mountains of New Hampshire and the Green Mountains of Vermont. On Whiteface Mountain in New Hampshire, it was estimated that between 20% and 70% of the Red Spruce trees were showing signs of die-back.

As a consequence of these observations, the United States Government funded an investigative programme called the National Acid Precipitation Assessment Programme which was concluded in 1990. One of the conclusion of this report was that acid rain was not a major cause of plant death. The only trees that were damaged in the US belonged to one species growing at the highest altitudes, i.e. at the limit of their growing range.

In Europe, it was found that forest decline took more than one form and was caused by a variety of reasons. Plant life nearest to the source of pollution will be damaged if the level of pollution is sufficiently high, which is rare in Western Europe. Acid rain was found to contribute to magnesium leaching (an essential plant trace element) in some forest areas but this could easily be redressed by the application of fertiliser. The areas where die-back was worst did not coincide 100% with areas of high acidity. There is thus controversy over the involvement of acidification in forest damage.

Acid rain also does not appear to have any significant effect on crops. Other factors have been found to be important such as agricultural practises, soil type and climate. For example, fast growing conifers leach out *bases* from the soil thus increasing its acidity at a far faster rate than acid rain does. When the trees are cut down, unless lime is added to the soil to increase its pH, then new plant growth will be adversely affected. Even if the rain is not acidic, the run-off from such soil will be, and if it enters an aquatic system can cause damage.

All types of water resources are very vulnerable to contamination by acids. Unlike soils they cannot as readily adjust to changes in their acidity. The consequences of an increase in acidity on the animals and plants that live in the water are often complex and difficult to understand. Amongst the many aspects to be considered is the actual life cycle of an aquatic organism. For example, fish fry are much more sensitive to their surroundings than are adult fish. The acidity of the water can be such that it interferes with the uptake of certain elements through the gills of fish as the water passes through them. This is the primary cause of fish fatality in acid waters and involves loss in nerve activity which ultimately leads to twitching and death. The most dramatic effect on aquatic systems is, in fact, the loss of the fish population. It has been reported that there are over two hundred fish-less lakes in the Adirondacks, over one hundred fish-less lakes in Canada and damage to many lakes in Minnesota. There are also thousands of lakes in Sweden at risk of losing fish populations because of excess acidity. Not only does damage occur through the direct deposition of acid into the lakes, there is also evidence that melting snow releases further large amounts of acidity which can interfere with spawning in the spring. What is interesting about these figures is that it is usually the smaller lakes and streams at higher altitudes that have a low pH. This is linked to their local geological and surrounding vegetation which, together with their limited catchment area, leads to acidification. Larger lakes have significantly higher pH's. There is no doubt that acid rain can directly cause problems but these are sometimes greatly enhanced by factors nothing to do with man's activities.

There is a wide range of fears and problems to be addressed concerning atmospheric pollution. How can the emissions of pollutants to the atmosphere be controlled?

THE MANAGEMENT OF AIR POLLUTION

To minimise air pollution an integrated pollution control approach can be used which attempts to reduce the release of pollutants. The approach currently in general use is the "best available techniques not entailing excessive cost" (BATNEEC) approach. Here the word "best" means the most effective technique or combination of techniques which prevents, minimises or renders harmless polluting emissions.

There are many ways of reducing emissions that can be selected according to the problem in hand. The polluting effects of solid particles (grit, dust, fumes) depends greatly upon the size of those particles. Particles that have been produced by mechanical operations such as grinding are usually large in size. These easily settle under the influence of gravity and are more easily controlled and therefore managed. Here, a process which depends upon the removal of a surface layer by a potentially polluting chemical might benefit by being replaced by a mechanical operation.

Volatile organic solvents which give rise to much fuming can be replaced with water-based ones. For example, water based glues/adhesives are much more environmentally friendly in being less toxic, less flammable, easier to store and more easily removed.

Halogenated compounds such as CFCs are being replaced with non-halogenated compounds such as propane and isobutane. Pump action valves which replace pressurised propellants in hair sprays and roll-on deodorants have become commonplace.

All of the above are examples of **replacement** and have been made in response to the effects of pollution. Another way of reducing emissions is to **improve** existing technology so that less waste is produced from a process, or to enable the return of useful "waste" to the process. For example, nitrogen monoxide is always formed in combustion processes but its rate of formation depends upon how fast the gases pass through the combustion chamber. If the temperature is kept below 1200°C, the rate of formation will become so slow that insignificant amounts of nitrogen oxide are produced.

A much more careful approach to the **monitoring** of a process can lead to better control of emissions. Here, we mean the optimisation of the process conditions to ensure maximum efficiency. In a combustion plant, for example, efficiency ensures minimum fuel usage and a corresponding reduction in pollution.

The control of air pollution is better started at its **source**. There are three main ways that this can be achieved. The first is to modify the processes involved so as to minimise the release of wastes to the atmosphere or to avoid this altogether. We have already looked briefly at some ways in which this has been done. The second method involves the collection of material in the form of particulate matter, and the third the absorption of toxic gases.

Particulate matter is separated from a gas stream by methods that depend upon the weight of the particles, by using a liquid to wash the gas, by using a fabric filter, or by electrostatic precipitation (c.f. Fact File 8.2). Whatever method is used, waste is still produced, albeit in another form. If particles are separated by gravity, scraped off fabric filters or removed from electrostatic precipitators then they have to be treated as solid waste and dealt with accordingly. Such is the legal demand in the UK on the control of particulate emissions that any inefficiency has to be dealt with immediately and stand-by plants are necessary in case of breakdown. The best available technique for removing particulate matter is normally selected. This decision is based on a review of several factors including the efficiency of the technique; the size of the particles to be removed; particle sensitivity to temperature; particle resistance to corrosion, electrical sensitivity, and moisture content.

Gaseous pollutants such as sulphur dioxide, the oxides of nitrogen and volatile organic compounds were once allowed to escape from tall chimneys, often as very corrosive and toxic plumes. Now such pollutants are treated according to the their type. Organic materials, for example, are often burned. If they have a commercial value they may be recovered by absorption in a suitable solvent and adsorption by a suitable surface. Inorganic pollutants are generally absorbed by water but this in turn generates waste water which requires a treatment plant.

The consequences of waste minimisation for air pollution are many. These include savings in energy, reduced costs of cleaning, the avoidance of pollution costs, reduction in the costs of control plants and their operating costs, and the avoidance of disposal costs for dealing with solid wastes or liquid effluents from gas cleaning plants. Clearly an integrated waste management approach is required so that problems generated by the treatment of wastes are not shifted elsewhere.

Often new research brings to the fore the identity of new and "unexpected" sources of atmospheric pollution. For example, in 1995 researchers at the University of California reported that fast foods such as hamburgers produced nine times more air pollution in Los Angeles than the city's bus service. It was claimed that the pollution was mainly due to grilling food which caused the fat from the hamburgers to drip onto the source of heat where it is burned at high temperatures. It has been estimated that fast-food restaurants produce some 14 tonnes of smoke and 19 tonnes of organic chemicals every day. These combustion products contribute to the infamous smogs of Los Angeles, and, it is thought that they could cause cancer and respiratory problems. Environmental officers in California are pressing for legislation to force fast-food produces to change their methods of cooking or install pollution control devices. On the other hand the producers and restaurant owners are challenging the researcher findings. Anyone for a barbecue?

**Figure 8.1 A Farmer Pollutes the Atmosphere - non-point or point pollution?
(Photo taken by the author)**

FACT FILE 8.1

Temperature Inversion The effects of air pollution caused either by the intentional or accidental release of materials to the atmosphere are normally greatly reduced by natural atmospheric mixing, i.e. by dilution. The degree of mixing depends on a variety of weather conditions, e.g. air temperature, wind velocity, and the movement of high and low atmospheric pressure systems and their interactions with local land formations such as valleys and mountains. Normally, the temperature of the air decreases with altitude. Sometimes a cold layer of air can settle under a warm layer and produce what is known as a temperature inversion. This results in the poor mixing of pollutants with air, causing an accumulation of the pollutants near ground level. An inversion can last some time if it lies under a stationary high pressure system and there is little or no wind.

Methyl Isocyanate Has the formula CH_3NCO and is a very flammable liquid at room temperature. It is a highly toxic chemical to humans as well as being a severe irritant. It causes pulmonary oedema (an accumulation of fluid in the lungs), asthma and nausea. It can react violently with other chemicals such as acids and strong oxidising agents.

The Atmosphere The atmosphere extends to a height of about 500 km above the surface of the Earth. Approximately 50% of the gases found in the atmosphere occur in the lowest 6 km and 80% within the first 10 km. These gases, together with suspended solid and liquid particles, interact with the surface of the Earth to make it habitable. There are two atmospheric layers of importance in terms of the effects of atmospheric pollution. The first is the troposphere which is the nearest layer to the Earth's surface, and extends up to a height of between 10 to 15 km depending upon the latitude and the season. This layer is heated directly by radiation from the Sun which penetrates the atmosphere. It is also heated by energy which has been absorbed by the surface and subsequently re-radiated as longer wavelength radiation. The thermal stability of the troposphere is responsible for global patterns of climate. The **stratosphere** is the next layer and extends up to about 50 km above the Earth's surface. In the troposphere, the temperature tends to decline with altitude. However, in the stratosphere the temperature increases with altitude, and may be as high as 0C. This is due to stratospheric ozone absorbing incoming ultra-violet radiation. The stratosphere exhibits none of the turbulence associated with the troposphere so any foreign material that is introduced will have long lasting effects. Exchange of material between the troposphere and the stratosphere is limited but it does occur, e.g. during thunderstorms.

FACT FILE 8.2

A **smog** is normally thought of as a mixture of smoke and fog. It is formed when the water content of air is high and it is so calm that smoke and fumes accumulate near their emission source. Smog reduces visibility and often irritates the eyes and respiratory tract. **Sulphurous smog** results from high concentrations of sulphur dioxide caused by the burning of sulphur-containing fossil fuels. It is aided by damp conditions and the presence of particulate matter. In highly populated urban areas, the death rate may rise considerably during prolonged periods of smog, particularly when a temperature inversion creates a smog-trapping ceiling over a city. Smog occurs most often in and near coastal cities and is an especially severe air pollution problem in Athens, Los Angeles, and Tokyo. Smog prevention requires control of smoke from furnaces and the reduction of fumes from all industrial processes. Smog has also been identified as being a consequence of the noxious emissions from motor vehicles and incinerators. The number of dangerous chemicals found in smog is considerable, and the proportions are highly variable. They include ozone, sulphur dioxide, hydrogen cyanide, and hydrocarbons and their products formed by partial oxidation.

Photochemical smog is a whitish yellow to brown haze, which irritates sensitive membranes and damages plants. This type of smog does not need either smoke or fog to form. It is formed when two of the primary pollutants, nitrogen monoxide and hydrocarbons, undergo reaction because of the energy supplied by ultraviolet and other types of radiation from the sun. The conditions necessary for this type of smog to form are the presence of the pollutants themselves, sunlight, a stable temperature inversion and land enclosed by hills. Petrol and diesel engines are regarded as one of the main contributors to this smog problem since they emit large amounts of unburned hydrocarbons and oxides of nitrogen.

Electrostatic precipitation involves the use of an electrical device for removing suspended particulate matter. It is a more expensive technique than mechanical collectors such as cloth filters but is much more efficient, particularly at removing very fine particles from a waste stream. The waste stream to be purified is passed over a series of electrodes which are suspended in the centre of the stream. These electrodes are supplied with a direct current voltage of the order of 50 000V and are referred to as discharge electrodes. At some distance from these discharge electrodes are placed a number of large metal electrodes which carry an electrical charge. These latter electrodes are the collector electrodes. The high voltage on the discharge electrodes causes the particles in the waste stream to acquire an electrical charge (ionise). The collector electrodes carry an opposite charge to those of the particles which are attracted to them and become attached to their surface. At appropriate times, the collector electrodes are washed or scraped clean to remove the deposit. This technique has been very successful in removing atmospheric pollutants from waste flue gases.

Further Reading Chapter 8

A.J.Chauhan et al, *Air Pollution, Past, Present & Future*, The Safety & Health Practitioner, May 1995

J.Fishman & R.Kalish, *Global Alert: The Ozone Pollution Crisis*, London, Plenum, 1990

S.Jasanoff, *Learning from Disaster: Risk Management After Bhopal*, Philadelphia, University of Philadelphia Press, 1994

D.D.Kemp, *Global Environmental Issues: A Climatological Approach*, London, Routledge, 1994

J.L.Kulp, *Acid Rain: Causes, Effects, and Control*, Regulation, Winter 1990, No.43

J. Simon (Ed.), *The State of Humanity*, Cambridge MA, Blackwell Publishers, 1995

J.McCormack, *Acid Earth: The Politics of Acid Pollution (3rd Ed.)*, London, Earthscan, 1997

R.Stolarski et al, *Measured Trends in Stratospheric Ozone*, Science, **256**, April 17th 1992

D.R.Varma & I.Guest, *The Bhopal Accident & Methyl Isocyanate Toxicity*, Journal of Toxicology & Environmental Health, 1993, **48**, No.4

CHAPTER 9

THE MANAGEMENT OF AIR POLLUTION: DRAX POWER STATION
a case of environmental concern versus profit

In this chapter, a power station is used to show how a company has tried to manage a system more effectively in order to reduce atmospheric pollution. The close co-operation between company and local interests is illustrated. The claims made for the operation of Drax in terms of its environmental impact are examined. Finally, cost versus environmental concerns are highlighted.

EUROPE'S FIRST ALL-GREEN POWER STATION

In February, 1996, the local York evening newspaper reported that the sixth and final *flue gas desuphurisation (FGD) unit* (see Fact File (9.1)) had become operational at the Drax coal-powered power station in North Yorkshire, UK. The importance of this announcement lay in the claim that Drax had begun operating Europe's first all-green power station. The new installations, costing some six hundred and forty million pounds, contained new pollution controls that would help to combat acid rain. Although the power station was burning 11 million tonnes of coal a year, sulphur dioxide emissions (the prime contributor to acid rain) from its chimneys had been reduced by over 90%. Surely this was the sort of event worthy of celebration and pride? After all, this was to be a long term solution to a long term problem.

To an extent it was, but because this "clean" electricity is deemed to be too expensive the power station faces the possibility of shutdown for hours at low electricity demand times such as during summer nights and at weekends. The new plant has added about one-fifth to Drax's day to day running costs. In addition, the operation of the FGD plant makes the power station less thermally efficient. It sends out to the national grid less electricity for each tonne of coal burned, which means it earns less income. Here is a very good example of the controversial conflict between environmental pollution effects and profits. Would you be willing to pay more for your electricity in order to have cleaner air and prevent acid deposition in places often many miles from where you live? It is hoped that Drax will be able to compete with the new generation of gas-fired plants when tough new environmental standards are introduced at the turn of the century.

The story of the Drax power station and the attempt by its managers to respond to environmental concerns illustrates well how an integrated approach to waste control can benefit the environment in several ways. So successful has the plant been in meeting and exceeding current environmental standards that it has been registered under the European Union's Eco-Management and Auditing Scheme - the first UK plant to do so. In this chapter we will use Drax to illustrate how an industry recognised its duty to reduce gaseous and other forms of waste emissions to the atmosphere. How it went about achieving that reduction will also be described.

DRAX IN THE 1980'S

In 1989, Drax was the largest coal-fired power station in Europe and generated some 4000 MW of electricity. It burned 10 million tonnes of coal per year and emitted about 340 thousand tonnes of sulphur dioxide into the atmosphere. It was decided to fit FGD equipment in order to remove this sulphur dioxide to a level which would not adversely affect the environment. The way in which it was to be done was to use approximately 500 thousand tonnes of limestone (calcium carbonate) in the form of a slurry to absorb the sulphur dioxide, producing a marketable side-product of approximately 800 thousand tonnes of gypsum (calcium

Clouds of water emitted from the cooling towers.

The FGD plant and the main chimney. A faint smoke can be seen.

A closer view of the cooling towers.

Barlow Mound.
On the right you can see where new ash is being added.

Figure 9.1 Drax Power Station (Photos taken by the author)

sulphate). Whilst the method was known to reduce atmospheric pollution in terms of sulphur dioxide, there were still serious environmental implications to be considered, for example, in the mining and transport of the limestone.

Up to 1986, National Power, or as it was then the Central Electricity Generating Board (CEGB), relied on the use of tall chimney stacks to prevent pollution of the local environment by the flue gases. Such stacks helped to dilute the flue gases by mixing them with air and also ensured their quick dispersal. Unfortunately, as indicated in the last chapter, these diluted gases were transported over both short and very long distances and became other nations' problems as acid rain.

The FGD process was selected because Drax was well sited in relation to sources of limestone as well as potential gypsum markets. There also seemed to be an adequate transport system. The FGD process was known to be very efficient in removing sulphur-containing pollutants from flue gases. The added advantage was that the resulting "waste" products are in the form of liquids and solids which are much easier to handle than gaseous wastes. Hence, an approach was decided upon which, though it didn't stop the production of sulphur dioxide, transformed the problem into a different kind which was more manageable and acceptable.

The decision to retrofit Drax with FGD plant was made in late 1986, and the detailed planning of the project begun. Right from the start, the CEGB made the very important decision that all government authorities, water authorities and other interested parties would be involved and consulted about proposed changes. This ensured that important issues of concern were identified, together with the measures that might be taken to reduce the effects of the FGD plant on local communities. Initial discussions in 1987 indicated that whilst there was support for the plant, local authorities were very keen to safeguard their environment from any possible consequences of the development. The CEGB thus decided to produce an "environmental statement" which was not a mandatory requirement at that time.

In order to allay fears on the part of the Local Authority over the selection of the FGD process as the best choice for Drax, officials were taken to Germany (then West Germany) and Austria to inspect power stations already operating FGD systems.

There was a great deal of concern expressed over the quarrying of limestone, since much of it at that time was quarried close to the UK's National Parks. The predicted extra quarrying required only amounted to about 500 thousand tonnes per year over the normal annual figure of about 120 million tonnes. Nevertheless, the CEGB decided that it would not use any limestone quarried from the vicinity of the National Parks, and that the limestone would be transported by rail.

The product gypsum also presented some problems. However, it was known that FGD derived gypsum was a marketable product in that it was already extensively used abroad to make plasterboard. CEGB investigations predicted a potential market for the FGD gypsum in excess of 2 million tonnes per annum. The identification of alternative uses for gypsum such as a grouting material, setting retardant in the cement industry, as a means of improving the quality of soil and as a fertiliser, all helped to support the selection of the FGD process. In case the gypsum could not be sold, the local authorities also required the selection of an appropriate disposal site. After careful negotiation, agreement was reached to use a disposal site which would take the total gypsum production from Drax initially for a period of five years.

Major concerns were expressed by the local authorities over the transport of limestone and gypsum by road. As indicated earlier, the CEGB wanted all materials to be normally transported by rail. However, a study was made of the operational and environmental implications of an increase in the amount of transport, involving all interested parties together with a specialist transport consultant. The conclusion was that providing the main bulk of the limestone and gypsum were transported by rail, then any additional transport demands caused by the introduction of the new plant could easily be met by the existing roads. Despite this conclusion, much opposition still came from a number of local authorities.

This opposition was mainly fuelled by the concerns expressed over the number of major roads that would be have to be used which passed through several small towns. It had already been noted that attraction of new industry into the area had resulted in an increase in traffic. This, together with a natural growth in local traffic (e.g. domestic car owners), was seen to have already placed a sufficient load on the roads. The Drax power station was not, as it was operating then, considered to be a major source of local traffic. It was deemed to be a potential threat in this respect should the FGD plant go ahead. (The coal was already being transported by rail from the nearby Selby coalfield.) It was suggested that the answer to this problem was to build a link road from the power station to the local motor-way system. The CEGB studied the potential operational and strategic benefits for Drax as a whole and, taking local opinion into account, agreed to finance the cost of building the road.

Noise and dust were suggested to be a potential source of pollutants. The CEGB carried out a survey of the existing background noise levels at the plant. This enabled the new plant to be designed so that an acceptable noise level would be produced. In order to reduce pollution by dust, the limestone and other storage areas, conveyors, etc. were to be covered. Problems over dust emissions from the new plant itself were not expected because of the preventative measures which would be built into the plant.

In addition to gypsum, it was also known that the FGD process produced a liquid effluent. This effluent contains traces of impurities which came from the burning of coal, and the limestone and the water used in the FGD cleaning process. The liquid would have to be treated to remove as much of these impurities as was reasonably practicable, before any of it could be discharged to a local water course.

In January 1988, the CEGB produced an Environmental Statement which, together with the formal application to build the FGD plant at Drax, was sent to both the Department of Energy and the local authorities. After further consultations and modifications, permission was granted by the Department of Energy in August 1988 to build the FGD plant.

In summary, the CEGB's approach in adopting the "environmental statement" enabled proper consultation to take place and the identification of local environmental key issues and concerns which were being expressed by a variety of bodies. It was an attempt at trying to predict the future based on the best information available at that time.

DRAX AND THE ENVIRONMENT IN THE 1990'S

If Drax power Station is considered to be a system and the environment its surroundings, then it is possible to examine the exchange of materials and energy between the system and its surroundings and to determine some of the resulting environmental effects. The purpose of the power station is to convert the chemical energy stored in coal to a more useful energy form, electricity. The conversion process is complex and involves the input to and output from the system of a number of materials (cf. Figure. 9.2 and Table 9.1).

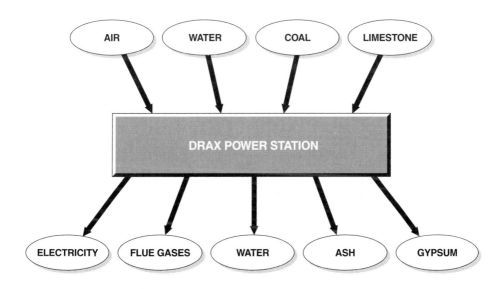

Figure 9.2 Schematic diagram of main energy and materials exchanges between Drax Power Station and the environment.

Air is extracted on site from the atmosphere and provides the oxygen necessary for the FGD process and for the furnaces. Coal is the fuel which is burned in the furnaces to provide the necessary heat to convert water to high temperature steam for the turbines which generate the electricity. Both limestone and coal are transported to Drax by rail. Water is extracted directly from a nearby river. The electricity leaving the power station enters the National Grid. Waste water is produced in a number of ways and has to be treated before it can be returned to the river. The large amounts of ash removed from the boiler and the flue gases are taken off site and used for as variety of purposes. Gypsum is also transported away and used mainly for the manufacture of plaster board. Treated cool flue-gases are released to the atmosphere via tall stacks. How are all these inputs and outputs related and how have the environmental effects been minimised? In order to answer this question, it is necessary to examine more closely what main processes occur in the power station.

The main parts of the power station are the furnaces and boilers. Here pulverised coal and hot air are fed to furnaces which heat the water in the boiler to form very hot steam. The burning of the coal produces large quantities of carbon dioxide. This, as we have seen earlier, is reputed to be a "greenhouse" gas and therefore a polluter of our atmosphere. In order to reduce the amount, more efficient generators will need to be developed which would reduce the amount of coal needing to be burned. The furnace contains low NO_x burners which are used to reduce the pollution of the atmosphere by the oxides of nitrogen. The super-heated, pressurised steam is fed to the generators and electricity is produced.

To prevent damage to the boilers, very pure water is required. About 160 million litres of water a day are taken out of the local river. This has to pass through a water treatment plant to remove dissolved gases and solids before it can enter the boilers. The water effluents from the FGD plant itself also have to be treated before they can be returned to the river. River water is also used to cool the steam leaving the turbines when it longer contains enough energy to generate electricity. The river water is first cleaned using screens, *flocculation* processes, sedimentation tanks, and chemicals to remove organic material. After use as a coolant, this warm water is sent to the familiar cooling towers before being recycled as a coolant again. After all this use, about 80 million litres of treated water are returned to the river each day. Careful monitoring of its quality is carried out to ensure that it complies with agreed standards.

For every 100 tonnes of coal that is burned about 16 tonnes of ash is produced in the furnace. The ash is produced in two forms. The first is called furnace bottom ash (FBA) and forms about 70% of the total ash formed. This is washed out of the bottom of the furnace with water. The slurry is sent to settling pits where the ash sinks to the bottom, is collected and eventually used to make building blocks. Again this water has to be treated before it is allowed to enter the local river. The other 30% of ash is called pulverised fuel ash (PFA) and comes from the use of electrostatic precipitators on the flue gases from the FGD plant. Once it has been knocked off the precipitators, this ash is mixed with a little water prior to being taken away for disposal. Most of it is used for land reclamation but its other uses include lightweight building blocks, infill for roads and the manufacture of some concrete structures.

About one million tonnes of PFA are produced each year. This is sent to a local derelict land reclamation scheme (Barlow, to the north-west of Drax) which involves the construction of a mound. The PFA is deposited in preordained positions, and to a calculated height. To stabilise the deposition it is coated with a vinyl product and it is sprayed green to improve its visual appearance. The water that is drained off the site enters the local water course but it is monitored closely to ensure its quality. The mound has been planted with grass and both woodland and agricultural areas established. Animals that graze on the mound and plants that grow on it are regularly tested.

MANAGEMENT STRATEGIES FOR THE CONTROL OF ATMOSPHERIC POLLUTION

It is clear from the above account that how air pollution is controlled depends upon a number of factors, e.g. the country involved, the nature of the pollutants, current scientific knowledge, whether the method adopted is short term or long term. The way in which control is brought about is a complex process which is effected by a number of approaches.

Table 9.1 The Input and Output of Energy and Materials to the Drax Power Station

INPUT	SOURCE	AMOUNT	NOTES
Water	River	160 million litres per day	Possible effects on fish and fauna particularly in draught conditions.
Coal	Mine	36 000 tonnes per day maximum	Produces the "greenhouse" gas carbon dioxide.
Oxygen	Air	At least 87000 tonnes per day (based on assumption that coal is 90% carbon)	Used in burning of coal - produces carbon dioxide
Limestone	Quarry	340 tonnes per day	Produces gypsum

OUTPUT	SOURCE	AMOUNT	NOTES
Electricity	Turbine	4 000MW	To the National Grid
Gypsum	FGD Plant	800 000 tonnes per year	Sold for plasterboard, etc.
Water	Cooling towers, water treatment plant	80 000 litres per day	Returned to river. Purity and temperature strictly controlled.
Ash	Furnaces and FGD plant	6 000 tonnes per day	Up to one million tonnes used per year for land reclamation.

OUTPUT	SOURCE	AMOUNT	NOTES
Sulphur dioxide	Burning of coal - not cleaned from flue gas.	At least 85 tonnes per day.	Continues to contribute to acid rain?
Carbon dioxide	From the burning of coal in the furnaces.	About 120 000 tonnes per day based on coal containing 90% carbon.	"Greenhouse" gas.
Nitrogen oxides	Burners in the furnaces.	?	50% reduction due to type of burners used

The first method is to identify what is the acceptable level of air pollution for a particular pollutant out of doors and not to exceed the legal limits. This is often termed "managerial strategy" and involves the determination and specification of air quality **standards** or **goals**. These can vary considerably from country to country, within a national or regional boundary or according to local conditions such as topography, climate, land availability and so on. Standards of air quality are derived from scientific investigations on the effects of individual pollutants on human health, plants, animals, building materials, etc and are based on the best techniques available at the time. Such standards can be greatly affected by economic, social, technical and political considerations. It may be that a certain level of sulphur dioxide in the atmosphere has been deemed to be the maximum that should be tolerated but national economic factors may prevent its implementation. Once standards are set and become legally binding then appropriate effective and efficient monitoring systems must be put in place. It is not possible to monitor every process all the time in every part of the UK, nor is the equipment always accurate and up to the task. One of the difficulties involved in setting standards is to provide a base line from which to make measurements, since zero levels are not practicable. What has to be done is to take an audit of what is being emitted from current known sources so that the success of subsequent control methods can be assessed. Where there are a large number and variety of contributing sources it is not possible to determine all pollution levels from all sources. All that can be done is to determine an approximate overall figure. In the case of Drax, the sulphur dioxide emissions were very large and could be determined.

Attempts have been made to provide mathematical models based on pollutant emission inventories under varying weather conditions which were intended to enable calculation of and predictions about air pollution levels. Unfortunately, the large number of factors which these models had to take into account have led to suspicion about their value.

Once the problems of setting standards and goals have been solved, how they are to be attained has to be addressed, i.e. the identification of methods of emission control available for use. This is a vital stage in the approach because the more options there are available, the more flexible the process of management can be. In the case of Drax, energy supply, transportation, land use, materials supply and the development of the site were all comprehensively examined from the point of view of pollution control options.

Whilst it is true that the enforcement of standards can reduce pollution to an acceptable (but not always a safe!) level, it can work in reverse. A company, for example, may for financial reasons be able to increase its profits by allowing a pollutant to rise to that acceptable level. To combat this, some countries have applied regulations which are designed to prevent any significant changes to pollutant levels in some particular areas. In the UK, pollution standards have been applied nationally without reference to a specific area - this has prevented, for example, the unfair treatment of companies who produce identical kinds of waste. Other countries such as the USA have a two tiered system, where pollutants are separated into those described as involving air quality standards and those of a more dangerous kind listed under emission standards.

The second method of air pollution control is based on the definition of the maximum amount of a pollutant which is allowed from a given source. In the UK, the approach for many years was based on the use of the Best Available Technology Not Entailing Excessive Costs (BATNEEC) approach. This is shown by the amount and variety of regulations in existence. Some specify the maximum allowed amount of a specified pollutant in a particular gas stream or the maximum amount of a particulate matter in a smoke, thus leading to a specification for the types of control devices that are used. Other legislation controls the type of fuel that can be burned (smokeless zones) or limits the amount of lead that can be put in petrol. This sort of approach is easy to apply and is often aimed at sources that emit a large amount of a single pollutant. This method is limited by current scientific thinking and knowledge.

The third approach involves economic control. Here, financial reward is given, or penalties are imposed. Very often potential polluters are charged according to the amounts of materials emitted if they exceed the permitted emission levels. This means that for as long as pollution continues the people who have caused it have to pay. Taxes and other levies have also been used to inflict a financial penalty. The money collected can be used to repair any damage, develop new pollution control systems or pay compensation to victims. The problem here is that such costs incurred by a manufacturing firm can be passed on to the consumer.

The final method is based on a "What is the cost?"/"What are the benefits?" approach. The total cost of all methods of controlling the pollution is calculated. This includes the cost of the equipment fitted, the cost of employing staff to run and control it, and administration. In addition to this, the costs of the damage caused by the pollution are assessed and include such things as premature death, illness, crop damage. The object of good "housekeeping" would be to minimise the sum of the two figures.

No single method is the answer to most air pollution problems - to minimise costs and maximise benefit for the environment, a combination of control strategies should be used.

DRAX, JULY 1996 TO JANUARY 1998

In July 1996 the local York evening newspaper announced that Drax was to burn coke with a high sulphur content. According to this report, Drax was planning to burn up to one million tonnes of a type of petroleum coke imported from the USA. The coke is a waste product from an oil refining process. The coke would be brought by sea to the River Humber ports and transported by road to Drax.

The coke contains some 6% by weight of sulphur compared with the 1% contained by the Selby coal. It has never been burned in a British power station before. The plan was to mix the coke with the coal until a sulphur content of about 1.7% was achieved. This would reduce the amount of coal being used but still produce sulphur dioxide emissions below the current emission standard.

Why? In order that the power station can compete financially with gas! Industrialists are often blamed for placing profit in front of all other concerns but in this case perhaps it is you, the consumer who is to blame. The question must again be asked, are **you** willing to pay more for your electricity in the knowledge that you are indirectly helping to prevent atmospheric pollution and reduce waste emissions?

In January 1998, the six flue gas desulphurisation units were shut down after cracks were discovered in the fans designed to drive the gases into the clean-up plant. Drax was also seeking Government permission to raise its annual level of sulphur dioxide emissions, so that it could continue to produce electricity at a reasonable cost.

FACT FILE 9.1
The Flue Gas Desulphurisation (FGD) Process
Chemically this process involves the conversion of limestone (essentially calcium carbonate, $CaCO_3$) to gypsum (calcium sulphate, $CaSO_4$) via chemical reaction with sulphur dioxide (SO_2). Inside tall absorber towers, a limestone/water slurry is sprayed continuously down through the flue gases emitted from the burning of coal in the power station boilers. The sulphur dioxide gas is absorbed by this slurry where it reacts with the calcium carbonate to initially produce calcium sulphite ($CaSO_3$):-

$$CaCO_3 + SO_2 = CaSO_3 + CO_2$$

At the same time, compressed air is pumped in at the base of the tower and the calcium sulphite is oxidised by the oxygen in that air to form calcium sulphate:-

$$2CaSO_3 + O_2 = 2CaSO_4$$

As crystals of gypsum are formed, they are separated from the water in hydrocyclones. Any moisture then remaining is removed in centrifuges.

Further Reading Chapter 9

R.Baty & E.East, *Environmental Issues arising from Flue Gas Desulphurisation*, Investigation of Air Pollution Standing Conference, Birmingham, 1989

Drax: Coal Fired Power Station, London, National Power PLC, 1995

Drax Power Station: Various Information Brochures, London, National Power PLC, 1995-97 : e.g. *Barlow Landscape Reclamation Scheme*

Eight Page Drax FGD Souvenir, National Power News, March/April 1996

R.E.Hester & R.M.Harrison (Eds.), *Air Quality Management*, Cambridge, Royal Society of Chemistry, 1997

R.E.Hester & R.M.Harrison (Eds.), *Air pollution & Health*, Cambridge, Royal Society of Chemistry, 1998

Open University Course team, *Air Quality Management*, T237, Units 14-16 Environmental Control & Public Health, Milton Keynes, Open University Press, 1993

CHAPTER 10

ENVIRONMENTAL MANAGEMENT
finding real solutions

The Precautionary Principle is explained and its importance emphasised. The relationship between the Precautionary Principle and the role of innovation is described, as well as how the former could impede the latter. Sustainability is explained in the context of environment, social development and economics. A framework by which environmental management can be carried out is described. The reader is also reminded of the new approach to the prevention of environmental misuse, the Life Cycle Approach.

INTRODUCTION

By now you will have read some examples of where things have gone wrong in the past. Since we know of these, surely we can prevent them happening again? The simple answer to this is probably "yes", but this way of managing our environment is remedial in nature and can lead to complacency and inaction. "It will be all right, we can take care of matters later!" is not the right approach or attitude to take. Having learned from previous mistakes we need to be alert to changes taking place in our environment, forward thinking and much more predictive in trying to plan for what might happen. We need to do the best we can at all times in the light of the best available knowledge however incomplete this might be. This knowledge will increase in the future, but for now action must continue to be taken to protect our environment from exploitation, which may cause potential irreversible damage.

What is needed is a better understanding of the processes that go on in our environment. If we can achieve this understanding, then we will be able to model these processes more accurately, and this may result in more reliable predictions and therefore more reliable, preventative action. The problem is that we do not know enough to act correctly for most of the time - there isn't enough data. Historical data is almost non-existent and extensive reliable monitoring over a long period of time hasn't been carried out. For example, had there been holes in the ozone layer prior to the discovery of the first one in the 1970's? Accurate observations and measurements over a long period of time are required, but this is of little use in the current situation or the short or medium term. There is also a lack of good modelling because of the very complex nature of the interactions that occur in the environment between a wide range of variables. Indeed, some scientists argue that perhaps what is going on is too complex to understand anyway.

THE PRECAUTIONARY PRINCIPLE

Because of the inadequate nature of both data and modelling, in environmental thinking a very important concept known as the Precautionary Principle has developed. This has challenged the usual thinking of government policy makers (civil servants and politicians) and scientists. Past experience shows that normally policy is changed only if there is a general consensus that something bad will happen unless policy is altered or evasive action is taken. The Precautionary Principle takes the view that the environment is so important that we cannot afford to make a mistake, and that action should be taken even if there is no consensus over a problem. It involves the idea that action should be taken in advance of scientific proof of cause and effect, on the grounds of wise management and cost effectiveness, i.e. it is better to pay less now than possibly more later. It suggests that resources, whether animal, vegetable or mineral, should not be "worked out" since we cannot predict what the outcome would be if all or too much of anything were to be removed from the environment. Great care needs to be exercised in the management of environmental change. It is not possible, for example, to predict all the consequences of decommissioning a nuclear power station. Hence, to convince the public that the processes being used are reliable and safe requires very sensitive management skills. The Precautionary Principle also places responsibility on companies or others whose actions may affect the environment to prove that what they are doing will not cause harm.

The Precautionary Principle is enshrined in the basic treaty of the European Union - the Maastricht Treaty signed in 1992.

> *"Community policy on the environment shall aim at a high level of protection taking into account the diversity of situations in the various regions of the community. It shall be based on the precautionary principle and on the principles that preventative action should be taken, that environmental damage should as a priority be rectified at source and that the polluter should pay."*
> **(Article 130r Maastricht Treaty)**

This would appear to be a very clear statement of intent. However, it leaves an important question unanswered, i.e. "How do we decide that a problem is both of sufficient gravity and sufficiently likely that society should take action?" If and when that question is answered another one naturally follows, "How much are we prepared to sacrifice in order to avoid the problem?".

Clearly, the whole concept of the principle says that in answering the first question we should avoid the extreme of "absolute certainty". Since very little in life is "absolutely certain" (except death and taxes, as Benjamin Franklin once wrote) there is general agreement that "beyond reasonable doubt" is sufficiently close to "absolute" for all practical purposes. This degree of certainty is what is required in a court of law in the UK for a criminal to be convicted. So, the Precautionary Principle implies that we need not be so certain. But just how certain?

Some people take the view that if there is any chance at all of a problem occurring, then we should avoid doing whatever might cause the problem. Our planet is a wonderful object, full of beauty and able to provide everything that we need for living a perfect, stress-free life. We must make "absolutely certain" that nothing is done that might harm the planet for our own use or for those who come after us. We must take no risk with our world! At first sight this can appear to be a very comfortable and safe position. In fact it is an extremely dangerous position and can be a recipe for not doing anything new. There is an implied (and sometimes stated) concern that modern life, with its industry, transport and consumer goods, has changed matters for the worse and that we must return to the ideal of life in former times.

The world is not like the idyllic picture just painted - it never has been. Diseases and deprivation have always been the lot of most of humankind. One of the most direct measures of the improvements that have been made is to look at the crude average life expectancy of people in the UK over time (c.f. Table 10.1). From 1840 to 1997 it has almost doubled. This is not to say that everything today is perfect, far from it. Statistics such as these say nothing about the differences between the various classes in our society, that the richer one is the more likely one is to live longer. There are areas of life that continue to need improvement.

If we look at the crude average life expectancy and infant deaths in some countries around the world (c.f. Table 10.2), it is clear that people do not share the good quality of life that we have in the UK. Why is this and what can be done about it? Water and food are the first two requirements in many countries. Sometimes these essentials are not available because of famine, corruption, terrorism or war. Outside of these deplorable situations, the most essential requirement is for clean water. More children die because of unhealthy water than from any other single cause.

Table 10.1 Crude Life Expectancy at Birth for England & Wales for both Sexes

YEAR	AGE
1841	41
1901-1910	52
1950-52	70
1987-89	75
1997	77

Adapted from The Health of the Nation, 1991, HMSO, London)

Table 10.2 Life Expectancy and Infant Deaths for some Selected Countries

COUNTRY	Life expectancy for both sexes at birth, 1997	Infant deaths per 1000 births, both sexes
Canada	79.3	6.0
Mexico	74.0	23.9
United States	76.0	6.6
Brazil	61.4	53.4
Chile	74.7	13.2
Ecuador	71.4	33.4
Guatemala	65.6	49.2
Austria	68.3	6.1
Belgium	77.2	6.3
Denmark	77.4	4.8
Germany	76.1	5.9
Italy	78.2	6.8
Poland	72.2	12.3
Russia	63.8	24.3
Switzerland	77.8	5.4

COUNTRY	Life expectancy for both sexes at birth, 1997	Infant deaths per 1000 births, both sexes
UK	76.6	6.3
Bangladesh	56.3	100.0
India	60.2	69.2
China	70.0	37.9
Japan	79.7	4.4
Pakistan	58.8	95.1
Syria	67.4	38.8
Egypt	61.8	71.0
South Africa	56.3	53.2
Australia	79.6	5.4
New Zealand	77.3	6.5

From US Bureau of the Census International Data Base

A similar situation used to exist in the UK (c.f. Chapter 6). Once the need for clean water was understood, in the mid-1800's people began to build sewage systems and water purification systems. Today, water is purified before we drink it by the addition of a chemical called *sodium hypochlorite.*

Sodium hypochlorite is made by reacting chlorine gas with *sodium hydroxide.* Chlorine is present in dioxins (c.f. Chapter 2). We have already reviewed the uncertainty concerning the toxic nature of dioxins and human beings. We do know that dioxins cause cancers In certain mammals. We do know that in humans dioxins at high doses cause a very unpleasant form of acne which is not life threatening. Some people invoke the Precautionary Principle and argue that because dioxins might cause cancer and other serious illnesses and since dioxins cannot be formed if there is no chlorine available, then chlorine-making should be banned. Such a decision would probably mean no sodium hypochlorite. Not only would we then make no progress in improving the water quality of developing countries, we would probably see a fairly quick reduction in the quality of drinking water in the developed countries. We know from historical, medical and scientific data that stopping water chlorination would lead to a dramatic increase in childhood disease and death. We do not know if dioxins actually cause human cancer or other serious illnesses - if they do the incidence is very low. Given these facts it would surely be folly to ban the manufacture of chlorine (c.f. Fact File 10.1). This is not to say that we should leave everything as it is today. Certainly we must continue to study the possible health effects of dioxins; clearly we should take steps to destroy them where this can be done cost effectively; clearly chemical reactions that might create dioxins as by-products should be controlled so that this does not happen to any significant degree.

In other words, the Precautionary Principle should lead us to take responsible and sensible precautions in a situation such as this where there is some probability of serious harm. To use legal language again, "on the balance of probabilities" there is a likelihood of human harm at sufficiently high concentrations of dioxins; it is therefore right to take reasonable precautions.

There appears therefore to be no simple answer to the questions we posed above ("How do we decide that a problem is both of sufficient gravity and sufficiently likely that society should take action?" and "How much are we prepared to sacrifice in order to avoid the problem?"). Every case must be considered on its merits. The standard of proof, however, is probably similar to that which occurs in a civil court ("the balance of probabilities") rather than that used in the criminal court ("beyond reasonable doubt").

Taking this pragmatic view is not opting out as some might argue; it is being realistic. It is admitting that environmental matters are extremely complex and decisions are extremely difficult. Decisions cannot be taken in isolation, there are often a wide variety of knock-on effects to consider. Using the Precautionary Principle requires evidence that serious and irreversible damage might occur, and a cost-benefit analysis of the different problem-solving options available.

THE ROLE OF INNOVATION

The Precautionary Principle, if applied incorrectly, can impede innovation. Innovation is a major force for the improvement and sustainable development of the environment. If we are to improve the lives of current and future generations then significant innovation is needed, especially in the area of eco-efficiency.

Since it is impossible not to affect the environment in some way no matter what we do, we need to develop new ways of reducing our impacts. In the case of waste management the key word, as stated earlier in this book, is minimisation. There is, remember, no such thing as zero waste, therefore innovative answers to how we can minimise waste and treat it so it becomes safe are required.

Innovation can take the form of well thought out processes such as the use of reed beds and other plants to make waste water and raw sewage safe for disposal (cf. Fact File 10.2).

Innovation can be about finding substitute materials. Copper, for example, is about the 25th most abundant metal and is regarded as a trace element. Its greatest use is for electrical wiring because of its excellent ability to conduct electricity. The demand for copper has steadily increased, resulting in the need for the exploitation of lower grade ores. This led initially to a rise in the price of copper and fears that we would run out of the metal in a very short time. Indeed, the consumption of copper at one stage, based on published known reserves figures, indicated that it might last for about a further 20 to 40 years. Had these latter figures been correct, and had society continued to use copper in the same amounts for the same purposes, then the fears would probably have turned into reality. However, what constitutes an available resource like copper depends upon a range of factors such as how much in

Figure 10.1 Reedbed Technology - Rosedale, N. Yorks (Photo taken by the author)

demand it is, how easy it is to extract from its ores, the economics of extraction, and the assumption that we have found every known reserve. In addition, copper is a metal which is easily recycled. Thus copper has in fact fallen in price in recent years. One of the greatest motivators for change is an increase in costs. As soon as this happens materials are looked for which can be substituted for those currently in use. So why don't we continue to use copper since it would appear to be both available and cheap? People have always looked for even cheaper alternative materials and ones that perform even better. Aluminium, of which there is no shortage, is being used to replace copper in certain areas of the electrical industries, as are optical fibres and microwaves for telephone transmission.

Oil, like copper, is classified as a non-renewable resource. We have been consistently informed that oil will run out one day. What has happened, and will continue to happen, is that the amount of easily accessible oil has decreased. Although oil prices are at an all time low in real terms at the time of writing, this can easily change. Certainly, the price of petrol continues to rise. Demand for oil is high and it is still a strategic material. Thus the search for new reserves continues, and those resources once identified as being too diffuse to be worthy of extract on economic grounds are being used. Because of the increase in costs and worries about how long it will last, people who want oil will be more economical in its use. Innovation is now occurring with the design of more efficient motor car engines, new devices for the production of useful energy, and the synthesis of substitute fuels.

Long before the last drop of oil is extracted from the Earth, innovation will have removed our current reliance upon it.

Innovation can take the form of "designing" into a packaged product ways of minimising waste, which also take into account the options for the treatment of its waste. What technique is used to dispose of the waste at the end of the product's life depends on the nature of the packaging material. Changes can be brought about to the packaging or the product it contains so that, for example, there is an increase in its potential for recycling. Can the product itself be made to last longer? (Old cars are causing most of the air pollution in California, thus product durability is not always the best solution.) If durability and recycling are possible, are the steps taken to achieve these more environmentally damaging than the original packaging and contents from which the innovation stemmed? Such questions need to be addressed in order to make any progress in minimising environmental impacts.

It is clear that in waste management, innovation equates to adaptability. Any new waste management technology used must be able to respond to changes in both the product and the composition of its waste. Equally, the options available for the treatment of waste must be able to change so that environment impacts are reduced.

SUSTAINABILITY

Precaution and innovation go hand in hand in attempting to sustain our environment. Environmental managers must ensure that what is currently available to us from the environment and our consequent impacts are at least as they are now. The best environmental management will result in extending the longevity of natural resources, reducing environmental impacts, improve the quality of the environment, and ensuring a good standard of living for all living things, including mankind.

The way in which the idea of sustainability came about, which was linked with conservation, began in 1972 as a consequence of the United Nations Conference on the Human Environment held in Stockholm, Sweden. Perhaps the best known definition came about as a result of the formation of the World Commission on Environment and Development in 1987 (c.f. Fact File 10.3). The role of this commission (sometimes referred to as the Brundtland Commission) was to identify and promote the cause of sustainable development. The Commission defined sustainable development as "development that meets the needs of the present without compromising the ability of future generations to meet their own needs". It was appreciated by the commission that what constituted human need varied throughout the world and depended a great deal on the attitude, culture and values of a particular society. Similarly, what could actually be achieved depended on the current state of technology, the way in which societies were organised, and on the ability of the biosphere to absorb the effects of human activities. Hence, because of these complexities sustainability was recognised as being somewhat vague in that it can mean whatever you want it to mean at any time.

In 1992, an international meeting, the so-called Earth Summit, was held in Rio de Janeiro, resulted in Agenda 21,which called for sustainable and environmentally sound development throughout the world. One of the greatest concerns recognised by the Rio meeting was the place of waste generation and waste management in the control of impacts on our environment. An outcome of this famous meeting was that a set of objectives and actions was produced which were aimed at waste minimisation, maximising the re-use and recycling of materials, and ensuring the safe treatment and disposal of waste. In the meantime, Europe produced independently in 1989 a waste management strategy which was issued in the form of a framework directive in 1991. Other actions have followed, including the Maastricht Treaty of 1992 which defines EU environmental policy, the establishment of a European Environment agency and continuing EU directives aimed at managing resources and waste.

Economics, i.e. cost, is inextricably linked with environmental management. Economists have therefore played their part in trying to define what is meant by sustainability. Inherent in all definitions is that future generations should be at least as well off in terms of health and prosperity as the current generation. The economic view of our environment is that it is another form of capital. Sustainable development then becomes the maximum development that can be achieved without depleting the capital assets, i.e. the resource base, of a nation. What is the resource base of a nation? Many economists see this as being composed of four major components, man-made capital, natural capital (natural resources), human capital (a knowledge resource), and cultural and moral capital. If the idea of sustainable development in an economic sense is accepted, then any society must behave in such a way that future generations do not have to pay a heavy price. If this is not the case and what has happened was unavoidable, then adequate compensation for the costs incurred must be provided.

Though there are many economic views on sustainability, three levels can be identified. The first one is termed **very weak sustainability**. This requires that the overall stock of capital assets described above should remain constant over time. For this to be so, any one component can be reduced as long as it can be compensated for by an increase in another. This relies upon the idea that one asset can be substituted perfectly by another, all that is required being that the total result has not changed. The implication here is that the total loss of an asset could be acceptable provided that substitution allows the attainment of a required result. Conservation thus becomes a worry.

The second level is termed **weak sustainability**. It is assumed in this case that perfect substitution of one asset by another is not possible, and that the world cannot guarantee a constant stock of assets. The need to maintain species populations and other resource stocks within prescribed limits to ensure the ecosystem's stability and resilience is also recognised. In order to maintain the benefits human beings obtain from a healthy environment, what is necessary is the management of the environment so that it meets human needs, supports all the variety of living things, and enables the environment (system) to respond to changing conditions. It is recognised that a critical natural mass of these main assets must exist, and that the assets have to be preserved to ensure that the life of all species is ensured.

The final level is **strong sustainability.** In this case, advocates reject the idea of substituting one asset by another to balance the books. The importance of the **scale** of human activities and its effect on the health and integrity of an ecosystem is also recognised. Scale is defined in terms of the input of energy and materials into an ecosystem, and the output of materials and energy from it in the form of useless waste. An ecosystem's ability both to regenerate resources that can be put back into an economy and to withstand emissions is an important consideration. An economy should be run so that any environmental impacts do not cause the environment to become permanently damaged or unable to absorb changes. Strong sustainability requires that the natural capital should remain constant with time - it is in keeping with the Precautionary Principle. So much, then, for the definitions of economists.

Sustainability is not just about whether a product or action can evolve in such a way so that damage limitation can be achieved and the environment sustained. Sustainability also involves cultural, social and economic dimensions. On a perhaps more personal note, one of the major difficulties is that there are probably as many ways of viewing the World as there are people! Everyone has her or his own view as to what is valuable, worth saving or what currently needs doing. Different people have different interests according to where they live, previous experiences, economic state, etc. and will view the same problem in very different ways. What might be considered as environmentally damaging by one person is not viewed in the same way by another. The values of people will affect the way in which they behave towards the environment. What an individual does is crucial with respect to cumulative impacts. Environmental managers must therefore identify how they can cause people to change their ways. This is why it is vitally important that meaningful dialogue takes place between all members of society at all levels.

Economic factors clearly have a bearing on motivating people to respond to change. How much are people willing to pay to have an environment which is a healthy place to live in and is filled with a wide variety of living species? It is hoped that reliance can be placed on the development of the idea that the environment is worth paying for, that it is valuable. If this is not possible then charges must be made, e.g. landfill tax was introduced in the UK in 1996 to discourage the over-use of landfill as a waste treatment option. It may be necessary to impose other charges to enforce the perception that the environment is valuable. Such measures are being considered in terms of an increase in fuel prices, and the introduction of an aggregate/quarrying tax and water pollution tax. If this should happen then the charges must be set at a reasonable level in order to meet economic sustainability, and any law or regulation has to be enforceable.

In order to determine when waste management has become sustainable criteria or target setting could be used. However, it must be realised that this can only occur in the light of current scientific methods, knowledge and understanding of what is meant by sustainability. Over time all these will change. If we couple this with the complex nature of the economic, social and cultural aspects of waste management then we see that the achievement of sustainability will probably never be measured accurately, and will involve an ever changing set of targets. It is the attempt at trying to meet these targets that will be important.

A FRAMEWORK FOR ENVIRONMENTAL MANAGEMENT

As we have seen, there are many tools available for environmental management, for example risk assessment, Life Cycle Analysis, eco-auditing etc. Rather than focussing on these tools initially, it is important to identify what is needed first, and then to choose the right tools to meet those needs. All activities (products, processes, etc) can be placed against a framework of needs in that they need to be safe, legal, efficient in the usage of resources and the creation of waste, and to address society's concerns.

Safety for citizens, employees, employers and the environment is essential. One of the most important roles of the environmental manager is to manage risks and thereby to improve on safety levels. One of the more important tools used is risk assessment procedures as described in Chapter 2. It is a balancing act between the costs of improving upon safety and the advantage gained by achieving the improvement. It involves decision taking which can cause a great deal of conflict between the decision taker and other interested parties. This conflict can be "cured" in a number of ways. It can be done by the imposition of power, e.g. "I'm the boss, so that is the way it is going to be!" This obviously involves little or no discussion and therefore missed opportunities for a more successful resolution to a problem can occur. Conflict can be ended using specialist advisers, e.g. scientists, who can analyse the problem, model it, and present solutions. This often involves limited discussion because of the view that experts are always right so reducing the need for anyone else to be involved. Sometimes, though, and some would argue too often, scientists and other experts have been known to be wrong. The best way forward is probably the free and open discussion of ideas involving not just facts but also ethical and moral considerations. Good risk management involves not only scientific facts but also an appreciation of the so-called "gut-feeling", intuition and previous experiences, as well as taking into account people's worries. This should lead to enhanced communications between all interested parties, mutual understanding and respect. Thus by opening up the decision taking process for others to take part in, a sense of ownership will develop, as well as better understanding of why a decision has been taken.

It is important that all environmental managers work within both the spirit and the letter of the law. Laws should ensure safety and protection of person as well as the physical environment. Unfortunately, this has not always been the case. In 1997, a large chemical company in the UK was fined for allowing a leakage of *vinylidene choride* (VDC) into a canal. It was caused by a series of operational and maintenance errors which led to an estimated leakage of 50 litres of the chemical. The Environment Agency estimated that the levels of chlorinated hydrocarbons that were in the outfall to the canal reached 180 times the level that the company was allowed by the Agency. Here is a good example where the law was applied to remind industrial companies to comply with the law and to improve their environmental performances. Hence companies need tools and environment management systems to ensure legal compliance.

Environmental management must ensure the efficient usage of resources and the minimisation of waste. As indicated in Chapters 3 and 5, tools such as Life Cycle Inventory and Life Cycle Assessment are useful in this connection.

There are a wide variety of concerns, both real and perceived, shared by society about what can happen to them as well as to the environment. Dialogue between all interested stakeholders is again very important if solutions are to be found. This is particularly illustrated by the Brent Spar oil storage platform episode (c.f. Fact File 10.4). This platform, owned by Shell, has been moored in a Norwegian Fjord since 1995 after a public outcry forced this international company to reconsider its original plan to tow the structure out into the Atlantic Ocean and sink it in deep water. This was a consequence of governmental opposition in Holland, Germany and other North European countries, together with public pressure and an emotive campaign by Greenpeace. The great majority of scientific evidence suggested that sinking the platform in very deep water was the correct option. Is it possible that the general public, government officials, etc were not properly informed or did not fully comprehend this scientific evidence because of poor communications? People knew that the disposal method selected was by far the cheapest option. Because of its cheapness, was there the assumption that it must be the worst option and that this might set precedents? Does cheapness really mean putting the environment last? What ever the answers are to these questions, it is clear that the views and fears of everyone, whether they are based on emotion or fact, or whether they represent a single person or that of a large group, must be taken into account in decision taking. Perhaps more discussion and involvement with all interested parties before arriving at the selected option might have saved a great deal of trouble.

TAKING THE LIFE CYCLE APPROACH

Many of our actions in the past have had unintended consequences. Not all of the consequences could have been foreseen, but many could have. By taking a Life Cycle approach to any process, product, action, etc. then it may be possible to prevent the sort of results that have occurred in the past. The listing or taking of an inventory of material and energy inputs and outputs to a system, together with an evaluation of the effects this inventory have on the environment, should be very useful for finding real solutions to environmental problems. Much more detailed information is thus required and its proper application involves value judgement during the valuation process. The whole lifecycle of projects should be considered at the start, to minimise unpleasant surprises in the future, and to prevent the solution to one problem simply creating a bigger problem somewhere or at some other time else.

It is probably the best approach currently available for us to further our understanding of the impact that our actions will have on the environment. It also enables better comparisons to be made between various approaches, actions, products, etc, and can therefore lead to advantageous decisions being made. It is open to abuse in that individuals could use it to their advantage in showing, for example, that their product is better that of a rival.

Models developed in the Life Cycle approach must be practical ones which are able to be modified according to evolving and new information. Resource and pollution flows to and from the environment can be measured and accounted for, and recovery, reuse and recycling processes included. It can be as simple or as complex as is necessary as long as it leads to an understanding of environmental burdens and benefits. Economic factors as well as energy, materials, and pollution have also to be taken into account otherwise manufacturers, distributors, retailers would go out of business.

In conclusion, we must recognise that precaution must be applied to our approach in using the environment but not to the extent of causing stagnation to innovation or reduction in living standards. It is relatively easy to define ecological/environmental sustainability but there are a number of other aspects to be considered which makes the concept of sustainable development quite difficult to put into operation. Nevertheless, there are a number of valuable tools in existence which, when placed into a well thought out framework of environmental management based on a lifecycle approach, can enable much progress to be made in how we deal with our environment. It is possible to tip the balance away from wasting and destroying our planet's resources to ensuring their efficient use in a sustainable way.

FACT FILE 10.1

Chlorine gas is a chemical element with a rather bad reputation. It was used in its elemental form in the First World War as a poisonous gas, and in the manufacture of phosgene ($COCl_2$) another poisonous gas. In more modern times, it has been used to make chlorocarbons which are often toxic. Thus, the impression might have been created in some people' minds that all chlorine-based compounds are evil! In the UK in early 1998,the Chemical Industries Association launched an advertising campaign to give chlorine a better image and improve the public's understanding of the chemical. The campaign emphasised the use of chlorine in the manufacture of PVC (polyvinylchloride) plastic and its consequent use in plastic blood bags for blood storage and use in transfusion. Why? Because pvc is not biodegradable, without pvc there would be difficulty in packaging blood. Advertising the use of chlorine in the making of CD's was also designed to affect the public's view. Compounds of chlorine are very often used, for example, it is a component of the salt you put on your chips, and it is found in the bleach you put down your toilets. It is an important component of your blood, and plays an important role in the way your nerves function. Chlorine is vital in the manufacture of a whole range of items such as solvents, paints, dyes, detergents, plastics, tyres, etc.

FACT FILE 10.2
Using Plants to Clean up Water
Innovation 1

Reeds are wetland plants. Thus their root systems are in soil which is usually covered with water. The common reed *Phragmites australis* is used to treat domestic and industrial waste waters in the UK. A pit is dug which is then sealed at the bottom and sides with clay and/or a synthetic liner. Soil is then added and the reeds planted in rows. Effluent is then fed through pipes on to the reed bed. This effluent percolates through the soil to the root system. There, microorganisms degrade the organic components. Oxygen is fed to the roots via the leaves and hollow stems so that aerobic processes take place which convert the pollutants to harmless substance like carbon dioxide, nitrogen and water. A small amount of sludge is produced. Some anaerobic degradation also takes place.

In Rosedale, North Yorkshire, UK, in 1996, a sewage treatment plant was officially opened which uses reed bed technology to treat the domestic dirty water waste of about three hundred people. The reeds are about 2 metres high and present a pleasant view to the beholder. There is very little smell associated with the beds, which once set up have low running costs. There are no sludge disposal problems either.

Reed beds are also being used by a large chemical company in the North of England to remove organic pollutants from its effluent waste water.

Innovation 2

At Rutgers University, New Jersey, USA, scientists have developed a new way of cleaning up water which has been contaminated with *uranium*. They have been using sunflowers. These flowers have been found to reduce the amount of uranium in such water by as much as 95%. The uranium is absorbed by the roots of the plant and concentrated there. Negligible amounts of uranium are found in the stems of the sunflowers. The roots are dried and treated with acid. The acid dissolves the uranium, leaving behind a mass of plant residue which is no longer radioactive. The uranium is concentrated in the acid which can be then be easily treated. The technique has already been applied to a former nuclear processing plant in the USA, where it was found to reduce the uranium in effluents to below the US Environmental Protection Agency water standard of $20\mu gl^{-1}$.

FACT FILE 10.3
Some important dates in defining Sustainable Development

1972 The Stockholm Meeting. The International Union for the Conservation of Nature (IUCN) played an important role in developing the concept of sustainability. Led to the subsequent setting up of the United Nations Environmental Programme (UNEP), the Convention on International Trade in Endangered Species (CITES).

1977 The IUCN was commissioned by UNEP to prepare the document World Conservation Strategy. UNEP and the Worldwide Fund for Nature (WWF) both supply funding and input.

1980 The first WORLD CONSERVATION STRATEGY (WCS) was published which defined conservation as " the management of human use of the biosphere so that it may yield the greatest sustainable benefit to present generations whilst maintaining its potential to meet the needs and aspirations of future generations. Three main aims were identified, the maintenance of essential ecological processes and life-support systems; the preservation of genetic diversity, and ensuring of the sustainable utilisation of species and ecosystems.

1987 The World Commission on Environment and Development (WCED) produced the Brundtland report. The WCED was established by the UN in 1983.

1991 The second WCS publication "Caring for the Earth". This document had two main aims. The first was to produce a new ethic for sustainable living and to translate it into practice. The second aim was to integrate further conservation and development. This report gave a set of principles for building a sustainable society together with suggested actions that could be taken.

1992 The Food and Agricultural Organisation (FAO) of the UN defined sustainability as "the management and conservation of the natural resource base, and the orientation of technological and institutional change in such a manner as to ensure the attainment and continued satisfaction of human needs for the present and future generations. Such sustainable development conserves land, water, plant and animal genetic resources, is environmentally non-degrading, technically appropriate, economically viable and socially acceptable."

1992 The United Nations Conference on Environment and Development (UNCED) in Rio de Janeiro, Brazil (the so-called Earth Summit). It established a Convention on Biological Diversity, Framework Convention on Climate Change, Forest Principle, the Rio Declaration of 27 Principles, and Agenda 21. Emphasis was placed on developmental issues as this had a socio-political tone. Less emphasis was placed on ecological concerns.

AGENDA 21- Waste Management
Objective Number 1:The minimisation and prevention of waste.
- Waste is to be stabilised or reduced in quantity before being sent for final disposal.
- Procedures for quantifying the amounts and types of waste to be strengthened.
- Incentives are to be provided to reduce unsustainable production of waste.
- National waste minimisation plans are to be developed.

Objective Number 2 The maximisation of environmentally sound re-use and recycling.
- National re-use and recycling systems are to be strengthened.
- Policy procedures are to be introduced to encourage re-use and recycling of materials.
- By the year 2000 to have national programmes with targets set for re-use and recycling.
- Programmes to be in place which help to inform and make the public aware of the value of re- use and recycling.

Objective Number 3 The promotion of environmentally sound waste disposal.
- National waste management plans are to be developed.
- Waste management within a country's own borders is to be encouraged.
- The "Polluter Pays Principle" is to be applied to the disposal of waste.

FACT FILE 10.4
The Brent Spar Story

The Brent Spar was an obsolete oil storage platform that Shell no longer wanted. The company therefore came up with a range of ways for getting rid of it. After careful review, two options were selected and independently assessed to determine which one might be the best form of destruction from the point of view of protecting the environment. The first choice was to break it up or dispose of it on land, the second was to sink it in deep water. Eventually deep-sea disposal was selected. At this stage, Greenpeace commissioned its own independent report via an offshore engineering consultant, who supported the onshore method of disposal. One of the main objections to dumping at sea that Greenpeace made was that the platform tanks contained sludge which would endanger the marine environment if it eventually leaked out. Shell reported that there was only 100 tonnes of sludge on board which contained quantities of the heavy metals zinc and copper, together with much smaller amounts of cadmium, arsenic, chromium, mercury and PCBs. There were also some 30 tonnes of radioactive scale on board. Greenpeace claimed that this waste would cause irreversible damage to the marine environment and its lifeforms. Shell, as well as most independent scientific opinions, disagreed. They suggested that any contamination of the sea-bed would be negligible, very localised and inaccessible to the food chain because the platform would be sunk to a great depth. Shell also stated that the proportion of heavy metals in the sludge was not significantly different from that which would be present in the same mass of plankton or marine sediment. The radioactive scale was only as radioactive as the granite buildings in Aberdeen, Scotland, and would only be a hazard if it were dried and inhaled. This would happen if the platform were to be dismantled on land.

In February 1995, the UK government approved the sinking of the platform as the best possible environmental option. Its decision was circulated to other countries bordering on the North Sea. None of these countries opposed the plan at this stage. On the 30th April 1995, Greenpeace protesters occupied the Brent Spar. Further protests followed in Germany which included a public boycott of Shell petrol stations. Indeed, violence erupted in that petrol bombs were thrown at stations and threats of violence were made against Shell workers. At this point, the eleven countries bordering on the North Sea changed their position and called for a moratorium on the disposal of offshore installations at sea. The UK and Norway were opposed to this idea.

The hostile reception of countries, coupled with the safety problems associated with boycotts, and the presence of Greenpeace members on the platform made Shell shelve its immediate plan. Shell, it has been claimed, had set a precedent for an international company to bow to external pressure against scientific opinion.

By 1997, Shell had spent millions of pounds over two years on further discussions and the investigation of new proposals for the destruction of Brent Spar. Three methods were considered, (1) deep-sea disposal, (2) dismantle in a dry dock, scrap and recycle, (3) cut into circular sections to use as a quay extension and scrap the superstructure.

In January 1998, Shell decided that the platform was to be cut into ring sections and would become a quay extension at Mekjarvik in Norway. This represents the Best Practical Environmental Option (BPEO). Amongst the reasons given for this decision are that Brent Spar is starting from a new location, new specific re-use opportunities have arisen, and costs have changed.

Further Reading Chapter10

D.B.Botkin et al, Environmental Science: *Earth as a Living Planet*, Chichester, Wiley, 1995

R.Cobban et al, Spring Cleaning Industry, *Chemistry in Britain,* 1998, **14**, No.2

S.R.Dovers & J.W.Handmer, Ignorance the Precautionary Principle & Sustainability, *Ambio,* 1995, **24**, No.2

P.R.Ehrlich, Betrayal of Science and Reason: *How Anti-environmental Rhetoric Threatens Our Future*, Washington DC, Island Press/Shearwater Books, 1996

D.Hunt & C.Johnson, *Environmental Management Systems - Principles & Practice*, Maidenhead, McGraw-Hill, 1995

JG.Jones & G Hollier, *Resources, Society & Environmental Management*, London, Paul Chapman, 1997

C.Martin, Eco-taxes in the EU, *Chemistry in Britain*, 1997, **33**, No.12

M.Sanera & J.S.Shaw, *Facts Not Fear*, Washington DC, Regnery Publishing, 1996

APPENDICES, GLOSSARY & INDEX

Appendix 1
does size really matter?

Appendix 2
the unit of science

Appendix 3
parts per million

Appendix 4
classifying and naming living organisms

Glossary

Index

APPENDIX 1 - DOES SIZE REALLY MATTER?

Scientists believe that a reasonable estimate of the Earth's age is four and a half thousand million years. Another way of writing this age is 4 500 000 000 years. When dealing with such large numbers it is tedious to keep writing them out in such a long form so a shorthand method is adopted known as **scientific notation**.

In scientific notation 4 500 000 000 is written as 4.5×10^9, and we would say 'four point five times ten to the power of nine'. The raised number or superscript 9 is called a power. This power indicates that a number is multiplied by itself a certain number of times, e.g. 10^6 means that 10 is multiplied by itself six times:

$$10 \times 10 \times 10 \times 10 \times 10 \times 10$$

In scientific notation the number to be multiplied by itself is always 10 and therefore this notation is often described as the **powers of ten** notation.

Powers of ten are used simply because if we multiply a number by a power of ten only the decimal point needs to be moved.

For example, if 4.5 is multiplied by 10 the decimal point is moved one place to the right:

$$4.5 \times 10 = 45$$

If we multiply by 100 then the decimal place is moved two places to the right:

$$4.5 \times 100 = 450$$

Now $100 = 10 \times 10 = 10^2$, hence $4.5 \times 100 = 4.5 \times 10^2$ in scientific notation.

Multiplying 4.5 by more and more powers of 10 produces the following sequence:

$4.5 \times 10 \times 10 \times 10$	4 500	4.5×10^3
$4.5 \times 10 \times 10 \times 10 \times 10$	45 000	4.5×10^4
$4.5 \times 10 \times 10 \times 10 \times 10 \times 10$	450 000	4.5×10^5
$4.5 \times 10 \times 10 \times 10 \times 10 \times 10 \times 10$	4 500 000	4.5×10^6
$4.5 \times 10 \times 10 \times 10 \times 10 \times 10 \times 10 \times 10$	45 000 000	4.5×10^7
$4.5 \times 10 \times 10 \times 10 \times 10 \times 10 \times 10 \times 10 \times 10$	450 000 000	4.5×10^8
$4.5 \times 10 \times 10 \times 10 \times 10 \times 10 \times 10 \times 10 \times 10 \times 10$	4 500 000 000	4.5×10^9

The dinosaurs appeared about 200 000 000 years ago and the first birds about 165 000 000 years ago. If you wanted to calculate the difference in years between their respective appearances we would subtract one from the other:

$$\begin{array}{r} 200\ 000\ 000 \\ -\underline{165\ 000\ 000} \\ 35\ 000\ 000 \end{array}$$

It would be extremely tedious even with a calculator to do many calculations like this. We can simplify by using scientific notation!

Now $200\ 000\ 000 = 2 \times 10^8$ and $165\ 000\ 000 = 1.65 \times 10^8$. As long as the powers of ten are the same for both numbers then the power can be ignored when subtracting:

$$2\ -\ 1.65\ =\ 0.35$$

but must be reinstated in the answer as 0.35×10^8.

In scientific notation it is not usual to leave an answer in this form but to rewrite it so that one digit is to the left of the decimal point, i.e. 0.35 would be written as 3.5 and the powers of ten adjusted accordingly. This way of writing a number is called **standard form**.

To change 0.35 to 3.5 we multiply 0.35 by 10 and move the decimal point one place to the right. To compensate for having multiplied once by ten we must reduce the power by 1, from 8 to 7. Hence our answer in standard form would be 3.5×10^7. So the number of years between the appearance of the dinosaurs and the birds is 3.5×10^7 years.

Note the following conversions to standard form:

$$350\ =\ 3.5 \times 10^2$$
$$350 \times 104\ \ =\ 3.5 \times 10^6$$
$$0.35 \times 103\ =\ 3.5 \times 10^2$$

Creatures with a backbone first appeared some 4.65×10^8 years ago and the first man-like creature walked upright about 5×10^6 years ago. Clearly we have a problem with subtraction here because of different powers of ten. In longhand we could write,

$$465\ 000\ 000$$
$$\underline{-5\ 000\ 000}$$
$$460\ 000\ 000$$

In scientific notation we need to make both powers of ten the same - let us select 10^6. The appearance of the first creatures with backbones occurred

465×10^6 years ago and the first man-like being walked upright 5×10^6 years ago. We can now subtract one number from another,

$$465\ -\ 5\ =\ 460$$

which gives 460×10^6. In standard form this becomes 4.6×10^8 years.

In the above examples, the time periods are very long and the numbers expressed very large. What happens when we have to consider small periods of time? Very small numbers can be just as tedious to write as very large ones.

For example, if a tuning fork vibrates 256 times in one second, then the time it would take one vibration to occur would be one two hundred and fifty sixth of a second, i.e. one divided by 256 of a second. This can be written as;

$$\frac{1}{256}$$

or 0.0039 second

Another way of looking at the above number is to recognise it as being the same as 3.9 divided by 1000 or 3.9/1000. 1000 as we have already seen is 10^3 and therefore we can write 3.9/1000 as $3.9/10^3$ or $3.9 \times 1/10^3$.

Now $1/10^3$ is written in scientific notation as $1 \times 10-3$. This is pronounced as "one times ten to the minus three". The power depicted by minus three (-3) is the number of times we have divided the number by ten.

Some more examples are shown below.

1/10 000	$1/10^4$	1×10^{-4}	0.0001
1/100 000	$1/10^5$	1×10^{-5}	0.00001
1/1 000 000	$1/10^{-6}$	1×10^{-6}	0.000001

The number 0.0039 now becomes 3.9×10^{-3}, and the time for a single vibration is 3.9×10^{-3} second. In other words, the negative power tells you how many places to the left the decimal place must be moved to give the decimal figure.

Protozoa are typically 2×10^{-6} to 7.0×10^{-5} metre in length. If this is written in non-scientific form we would put 0.000002 to 0.00007 metre.

The addition and subtraction of such small numbers is carried out in the same way as for the big numbers described above. One major advantage of writing numbers like this for both big and small numbers is it makes calculations involving the multiplication and division of them easier to perform - but if you are interested in this have a look in a maths book!

APPENDIX 2- THE UNITS OF SCIENCE

The basic units of measurement in science are Standard International or SI units. The unit of mass is the kilogram (kg), the unit of length the metre (m), and the unit of time the second (s). In this book we have occasionally introduced you to some peculiar numerical values and units. Let us now try to explain what these mean.

The unit of mass in common use is called the gram (g) and is one thousandth of a kilogram or 1×10^{-3}kg. Sometimes the latter figure is simply written 10^{-3}kg.

The milligram (mg) is one thousandth of a gram or 1×10^{-3}g. The prefix "m" means one-thousandth part. This is equal to one millionth of a kilogram or 1×10^{-6}kg. The prefix "k" in kg means one thousand, so a kilogram is one thousand grams or 10^{3}g.

Smaller quantities of mass are measured in micrograms or "µg" where the Greek letter "µ" represents "micro" and means one millionth. The microgram is therefore 1×10^{-6}g or 1×10^{-12}kg. Even smaller masses are measured in "nanograms" or "ng". The nanogram is 1×10^{-9}g or 1×10^{-12}kg.

When dealing with volume, 1 m^3 is equivalent to 1x 10^{6} (or one million) cm^3. The litre (l), otherwise more correctly known as the cubic decimetre (1 dm^3), is 1000cm^3. Therefore, it is also equal to 1×10^{-3}m^3 since it is a thousand times smaller than the cubic metre.

The millilitre (ml) is often used, and means 1×10^{-3} of a litre, which is the same as 1 cm^3. The microlitre (µl) is also found in the literature and is equivalent to 1×10^{-6}l, or 1×10^{-3} cm^3, or 1×10^{-9}m^3.

Often in environmental monitoring, concentrations of aqueous solutions are measured in units of mgl^{-1}, µgl^{-1} and ngl^{-1}. Remember that a superscript which starts with a minus sign means "per", so that mgl^{-1} means milligram per litre.

mgl^{-1}	means milligram per litre	= 1×10^{-3}gdm^{-3}
µgl^{-1}	means microgram per litre	= 1×10^{-6}gdm^{-3}
ngl^{-1}	means nanograms per litre	= 1×10^{-9}gdm^{-3}
pgl^{-1}	means picograms per litre	= 1×10^{-12}gdm^{-3}

Hence, a solution containing 3.5 µgl^{-1} of cadmium contains 3.5 x 10^{-6}g of Cd^{2+} dissolved in 1 litre of solution.

In the case of atmospheric measurements mass/volume related units are again used, but since concentrations are usually so small the m^3 is used. Hence, the units used are:-

mgm^{-3} = 1×10^{-6}gl^{-1}

When dealing with solid materials such as soil, units involving only mass tend to be used. These are:

$mgkg^{-1}$ means milligrams per kilogram = 1×10^{-6} gg^{-1}

μgkg^{-1} means micrograms per kilogram = $1 \times 10^{-9} gg^{-1}$

$ngkg^{-1}$ means nanograms per kilogram = 1×10^{-12} gg-1

Soil which contains 12 $ngkg^{-1}$ of lead would be stated as "twelve nanograms of lead per kilogram of soil".

The prefixes which are used in SI units and their meanings are shown in the table below.

Table 1 Prefixes for SI units that are very small

FRACTION	PREFIX	SYMBOL
10^{-1}	deci	d
10^{-2}	centi	c
10^{-3}	milli	m
10^{-6}	micro	μ
10^{-9}	nano	n
10^{-12}	pico	p
10^{-15}	femto	F
10^{-18}	atto	a

Table 2 Prefixes for SI Units that are very large

MULTIPLE	PREFIX	SYMBOL
10	deca	da
10^{2}	hecto	h
10^{3}	kilo	k
10^{6}	mega	M
10^{9}	giga	G
10^{12}	tera	T
10^{15}	peta	P
10^{18}	exa	E

APPENDIX 3 - PARTS PER MILLION (ppm)

A convenient unit when dealing with both aqueous solutions and gaseous mixtures is the "part per million". It is convenient because it reduces cumbersome numbers to simple ones, is universally recognised, and is a characteristic of any volume taken from the solution or gas mixture in question. If, for example, $100cm^3$ of a sample of water was found to contain 25 ppm of cadmium the form of Cd^{2+} then $1cm^3$ or $0.001cm^3$ or $1000m^3$ of the same solution, assuming uniform mixing, would also contain 25 ppm of cadmium.

Now 1 litre or 1 cubic decimetre of water is the same as $1000cm^3$ or $1 \times 10^3 cm^3$.

One cubic metre or $1 m^3$ of water is equivalent to $1\ 000\ 000cm^3$ or $1 \times 10^6 cm^3$.

Hence, $1m^3$ is also equivalent to $1 \times 10^3 dm^3$ or $1 dm^3$ equals $1 \times 10^{-3} m^3$.

This kind of reasoning can also be applied to volumes of air.

If 1 g of cadmium was found in $1m^3$ of water then, since this volume of water equals $1 \times 10^6 cm^3$, the concentration would be expressed as 1g in $1 \times 10^6 cm^3$ or 1 part per million.

Now let us look at water containing a concentration $0.33 \times 10^{-3} g\ l^{-1}$.

This can be written as $0.33\ mg\ l^{-1}$, if we know that $1 \times 10^{-3} g$ is 1 milligram written as 1 mg.

One litre is the same as one cubic decimetre or $1000\ cm^3$.

A cubic metre is 1×10^3 bigger than a litre.

Hence, if we had a cubic metre of contaminated water we would have $0.33\ mg \times 1 \times 10^3$ of cadmium present, or 0.33×10^3 mg.

Hence in the water there would be $(0.33 \times 10^3 \times 1 \times 10^{-3})g$ or 0.33 g of cadmium.

We would report that this sample of water has a concentration of 0.33 parts per million or 0.33 ppm of cadmium.

A water sample which contains $0.33 \times 10^{-3} g$ of cadmium in $1 dm^3$ of water would also have a concentration of 0.33 ppm.

A similar approach is adopted for volumes of air, i.e. substitute the word "air" for "water" in the above example, and perhaps "ozone" for "cadmium"!

From appendix 2, in the case of aqueous solutions mgl^{-1} is also equivalent to ppm, whereas μgl^{-1} is equivalent to parts per billion or ppb. For solids, $mgkg^{-1}$ is equivalent to ppm, and μgkg^{-1} to ppb.

For the atmosphere, ppm are expressed with respect to volume measurements. Hence, $10^{-6} m^3 m^{-3}$ is ppm volume for volume (v/v) and is equivalent to $cm^3 m^{-3}$, while ppb (v/v) is $10^{-9} m^3 m^{-3}$ or $10^{-3} cm^3 m^{-3}$.

APPENDIX 4 - CLASSIFYING AND NAMING LIVING ORGANISMS

There are many millions of living things on our planet. In order to sort out the wide variety of organisms, biologists have organised several systems of classification. One in common use is the so-called **Five Kingdoms Model**. This is based on how the cells of the organism are organised and how that organism feeds. Cells have been found to be of two basic types, the prokaryotes and the eukaryotes. Eukaryotic cells have a distinct nucleus, but prokaryotic cells do not. Indeed, prokarytotic cells do not have any well-defined internal cell structure at all (organelles such as mitochondria are absent). Living things feed in three different ways. Some photosynthesise, some ingest their food, and some absorb their food. Based on cell structure difference and mode of feeding the following five **kingdoms** have be established:

	PLANTAE	FUNGI	ANIMALIA	PROTISTA	MONERA
Photosynthesis	plants			algae	
Absorption		fungi			prokaryotes
Ingestion			animals	protozoa	

Bacteria and blue-green algae have prokaryotic cells and are placed in the kingdom **MONERA**. The **PROTISTA** are diverse one-celled eukaryotic organisms, which live singularly or in colonies. **ANIMALIA** are multicellular and have their cells organised into different tissues, are mobile or partly mobile and digest their food internally. **PLANTAE** are multicellular, usually having cells with thick walls, and contain chloroplasts which enable them to manufacture their own food by photosynthesis. The **FUNGI** are muliticellular and digest food externally by absorption through the surfaces of specially developed tubes called hyphae which make up their body.

Each of the above kingdoms is subdivided further. It is probably better to start from the bottom of this division process and work up to the top. At the bottom of the process is that division called the **SPECIES**. A species is a group of organisms that resemble each other in many important characteristics. If they reproduce sexually then species interbreeding occurs, but different species cannot interbreed to produce fertile offspring. Species that cannot interbreed but share important characteristics are grouped into a **GENUS** (plural genera).

It is at this stage that we can introduce a system of naming organisms that is unambiguous and precise. Separate species are given a two-word name, this being referred to as the binomial system of naming. The first word starts with an upper case letter and is the genus name. The second word is an adjective and starts with a lower case letter. This second word is usually descriptive or geographically based. This system of naming was established in 1758 by a Swedish biologist called Carolus Linnaeus. Latin names were used because that was the language by which scholars communicated in those days. So humans were given the genus name of "Homo" (meaning man) and the species name "sapiens" (meaning wise) hence, Homo sapiens (wise man). The tiger lily is called *Lilium tigrium*, the lion *Panthera leo*, the domestic cat *Panthera catus*.

At its simplest, one or more genera are grouped into a **FAMILY**, families into **ORDERS**, orders into **CLASSES**, classes into **PHYLA** and phyla into **KINGDOMS**.

In the animal kingdom there are, for example, two phyla called the vertebrates and the invertebrates (those with backbones and those without backbones respectively). The phyla vertebrates can be further divided into five classes, mammals, birds, reptiles, amphibians and fish. Each class is then divided into orders, e.g. primates, then into families, then into genera, then into species. So a full description of a human and the common dolphin would look as follows:

	HUMAN	COMMON DOLPHIN
Kingdom	animal	animal
Phylum	vertebrates	vertebrates
Class	mammals	mammals
Order	primates	cetacea
Family	Hominidae	Delphinidae
Genus	Homo	Delphinus
Species	sapiens	delphis

GLOSSARY

ACTIVATED CARBON/CHARCOAL.
Charcoal that has been treated with an acid or some other chemical to increase its adsorptive powers. It is particularly useful in removing coloured contamination from, for example, sugar so that it is white when used.

ADIPOSE TISSUE.
A layer of fat just beneath the skin and around various organs.

ADSORPTION.
Not to be confused with absorption. Adsorption is the interaction between gases and liquids and the surfaces of solids or liquids, i.e. there is the concentration and adherence of one material to the surface of another. Desorption is the reversal of adsorption. Absorption involves the penetration of one material by another and is often accompanied by adsorption.

AEROBIC RESPIRATION.
Respiration which requires air (oxygen).

ALGAE.
A large group of essentially aquatic plants found in both fresh and salt water. They range in size from microscopic plants that form the green scum on ponds to the huge brown kelps more than 45m long.

ALUM.
Normally taken to mean the double sulphate, potassium aluminium sulphate, $K_2SO_4.Al_2(SO_4).24H_2O$, which is used as in the dyeing industry.

ALVEOLUS.
A sac-like structure one cell thick that protrudes from the end of a bronchiole. Each contains a network of capillary blood vessels that permit exchange of gases between the blood and the air.

AMINO ACIDS.
Organic compounds containing carbon, hydrogen, oxygen and nitrogen. They contain at least one carboxyl group (-COOH) group and at least one amino group ($-NH_2$). These acids are of great biological importance because they link together to produce proteins.

ANAEROBIC RESPIRATION.
Respiration which occurs in the absence of oxygen. The most important application of anaerobic respiration is in fermentation used to make beer and wines.

AQUIFER.
Sandstone or Limestone rock that, because of its porosity and permeability, can store water in recoverable amounts.

BACTERIA.
Simple unicellular microscopic organisms, usually classified in the plant kingdom. They lack a clearly defined nucleus and most do not contain chlorophyll. There are three typical forms rod-shaped (bacillus), round (coccus) and spiral (spirillium). Are a major source of disease in humans but many are harmless and beneficial.

BENZENE.
A toxic, cancer causing, colourless, volatile, sweet smelling and inflammable liquid. It has the formula C_6H_6 and is a product of petroleum refining. It is the simplest of a very large group of organic compounds often referred to as Aromatic Compounds. The molecule is formed from a hexagonal ring of carbon atoms, which is referred to as a benzene ring where ever it occurs. It is used as a raw material for the manufacture of many useful organic chemicals and as solvent.

BILE.
A liquid secreted by the liver. It is bitter to taste, is alkaline in nature and has a colour ranging from green to yellow brown. This liquid is stored by the gall bladder. It has two important functions in digestion. Firstly, the bile salts it contains breaks down fats so that they can be more readily absorbed, and secondly, it neutralises stomach acids. Bile also contains excretory products such as cholesterol.

BILIARY SYSTEM.
The organs and ducts by which bile is formed, concentrated and carried from the liver to the first part of the small intestine called the duodenum.

BIODEGRADABLE.
Capable of being broken down by the action of bacteria.

BIOSPHERE.
The name given to that part of the Earth's crust and surrounding atmosphere that includes all living organisms both animal and vegetable.

BRONCHUS.
A large air passage in a lung. Each lung has one main bronchus which originates from the end of the windpipe (trachea). This main bronchus then divides into smaller branches which in turn sub-divide further into bronchioles. Inflammation of the bronchi is known as bronchitis. This is caused by irritation from chemicals, pollutants or by a viral infection. Bronchitis causes many deaths each year particularly among the elderly.

CADMIUM (Cd).
A highly toxic non-essential (to living things) metallic element. Used in electroplating coatings to form a corrosion-protecting layer for steel and its alloys. Many of its compounds are also toxic and have little general use.

CARBOHYDRATE.
An organic compound composed of carbon, hydrogen and oxygen. Carbohydrates are a component of many different kinds of food. Examples of carbohydrates are the sugars such as glucose and fructose.

CARBON MONOXIDE (CO).
A colourless, odourless, poisonous gas. Often formed during the incomplete combustion of fossil fuels. Used in the manufacture of chemicals.

CARBON DIOXIDE (CO_2).
A colourless and odourless gas which is the product of complete combustion of fossil fuels and in respiration. It is vital to the process of photosynthesis. Used in carbonated drinks, fire extinguishers, and an inert atmosphere in welding. As a solid it is used as a refrigerant.

CARCINOGEN.
Any agent which can cause cancer in human beings, such as tobacco smoke, high energy radiation or asbestos fibres. Chemicals are the largest group of cancer forming agents. Polycyclic aromatic hydrocarbons (PAHs) which occur in tobacco smoke, soot, pitch and tar are amongst some of the more dangerous.

CHLORIDES.
Salts of hydrochloric acid (HCl). Many metals also combine directly with chlorine to produce chlorides.

CHROMIUM (Cr).
A metallic element. Used in electroplating to give a highly light reflecting surface, and in manufacture of many special steels.

CILIA.
Protruding hair-like filaments which beat in unison to create currents of liquid over the surface of cells.

CONTROL GROUP.
In testing the effects of a pollutant on a group of animals, one half would receive doses of the pollutant, the other half none. The latter half group is referred to as the control group. The two halves would be carefully matched in terms of age, sex, weight, etc. Comparisons would be made between the test group and the control group.

DDT (DICHLORODIPHENYLTRICHLOETHANE).
The first most successful man-made insecticide. Although not very toxic to man, it is to some living organisms it was not intended to affect. A persistent chemical in the environment. Now banned in most countries.

DIBROMOMETHANE.

A colourless liquid which is a chemical compound composed of carbon, hydrogen and the element bromine - its formula is $C_2H_4Br_2$. It is the reaction of this substance at the high temperatures experienced in the motor car engine with tetraethyl lead which results in the toxic volatile compound called lead bromide $PbBr_2$.

ENDOCRINE SYSTEM.

In the human being a body system of ductless glands that secretes hormones directly into the blood stream. These ductless glands are not structurally connected to one another. Examples are the thyroid gland located in the throat, which secretes thyroxine a growth hormone; the adrenal glands situated on top of the kidneys which secrete adrenaline to stimulate the nervous system; the male sex glands or gonads which supplies testosterone responsible for the growth and development of the male sex organs and male secondary characteristics.

EPIDEMIOLOGY.

The study of disease, such as cholera, plague, influenza, cancer, heart disease, etc in a population. The population is carefully counted, and each person is defined in terms of age, sex, race, occupation, etc. The incidence (number of cases in a stated period of time) and the prevalence (number of people who are suffering at any one time) of the diseases is determined.

EVAPORATION.

The process by which a liquid turns into a vapour. It occurs from the surface of the liquid at all temperatures below its boiling point.

FATS.

Organic compounds containing carbon, hydrogen and oxygen, but the proportion of oxygen in them is very low when compared with carbohydrates. They are oily, greasy, waxy substances which when pure are normally tasteless, colourless and odourless.

FATTY ACIDS.

The common name given to another group of organic compounds. Fatty acids contain straight chains of carbon atoms, with some side chains. They are acids and contain a single -COOH group. They can be produced by reacting water with fats under alkaline conditions. Acetic acid, found in vinegar, is one of the simplest fatty acids.

FOOD CHAIN.

A kind of feeding order. At the bottom are green plants (producers) followed by the herbivores (primary consumers) followed by the carnivores (secondary consumers). At every stage including the end of the chain, acids, bacteria and enzymes act to break down waste and dead matter into forms that can be absorbed by plants thus perpetuating the chain.

FLUORIDES.

The salts of hydrofluoric acid (HF).

FUNGI.

A wide variety of plants that cannot make their own food by photosynthesis. They include mushrooms, moulds, truffles, smuts and yeast.

GALL BLADDER.

A muscular sac found in the abdomen which stores and concentrates bile which it receives from the liver. Bile is used in both digestion and excretion processes.

GASTROINTESTINAL TRACT.

That part of the digestive system consisting of the mouth, oesophagus, stomach and intestine.

GLYCEROL/GLYCERINE.

A thick, syrupy, sweet liquid obtained by the hydrolysis of fats and oils. Used in the manufacture of cosmetics, plastics, explosives, foods and antifreeze. Formula $CH_2.CHOH.CH_2OH$.

HALONS.
Organic compounds containing one or two carbon atoms together with fluorine, chlorine, bromine, or iodine. They are gases and were widely used in fire extinguishers until banned in 1994. One example is halon-1211 or bromochlorodifluoromethane, $CBrClF_2$ (compare with methane CH_4).

HEAVY METALS.
The general term for those metals which have a density greater than 6 gcm^{-3}. The common ones often associated with environmental problems are cadmium, chromium, copper, mercury, nickel, lead and zinc.

HEPATITIS.
Inflammation of the liver caused by a viral infection. Symptoms include lethargy, nausea, fever and possibly jaundice. Recovery is usual unless accompanied by complications.

HERBICIDES.
Chemicals used to kill weeds and other unwanted plants. They can either be selective and kill only unwanted plants or non-selective and kill all vegetation with which they come into contact.

HORMONE.
Chemicals secreted in minute quantities by some living organisms that help to control such body functions as growth, and sexual maturity. In human beings, it is the endocrine system that secretes hormones directly into the bloodstream.

HYDROCARBONS.
Chemical compounds composed of the elements carbon and hydrogen only. Hexane is atypical example and has the formula C_6H_{14}. When burned in a plentiful supply of air such compounds provide a lot of energy and produce carbon dioxide and water vapour. Incomplete combustion can yield highly toxic carbon monoxide and unburned hydrocarbons.

HYDROGEN BROMIDE.
A corrosive gas of formula HBr. When mixed with water it becomes hydrobromic acid (a relative of hydrochloric acid) and is one of the reasons why exhaust pipes on cars become corroded and useless.

HYDROGENCARBONATES/BICARBONATES.
The acid salts of carbonic acid (H_2CO_3). Their aqueous solutions contain the HCO_3^- ion.

IGNEOUS ROCK.
Rocks that are produced by the cooling of the molten magma found deep within the earth are referred to as igneous rocks.

IMMUNE SYSTEM.
A collection of cells and proteins that work to protect the body from potentially harmful infections from micro-organisms such as bacteria and viruses. The system also plays a role in the control of cancer and is responsible for allergic reactions and rejection problems in surgical transplant operations.

INORGANIC MATERIALS.
Materials which do not include carbon in their composition. The exceptions to this rule are carbonates, carbides and the oxides of carbon.

INVERTEBRATE.
An animal without a backbone. Most are insects, but also includes molluscs, crustaceans and arachnids.

LEACHING.
The removal of soluble substances from soils by percolating water.

LIME.
The name given to both calcium oxide (CaO) and calcium hydroxide ($Ca(OH)_2$) - the former is known as "quicklime" and the latter "slaked lime". Quicklime is a white solid obtained by heating limestone. It is used as a refractory material, flux, in glass making, water treatment, food processing and as a cheap anti-acid. Slaked lime is a white solid made by adding water to quicklime. It is used to make mortar, plaster, cements, in water softening and in agriculture.

LIMESTONE.
A sedimentary rock. Composed mainly of calcium carbonate, $CaCO_3$. Formed from deposits of marine invertebrate skeletons. Used to make cement, lime and building materials.

MAGNESIUM.
A common metallic element used to make lightweight alloys. Many of its compounds are in common use, e.g. magnesium carbonate, $MgCO_3$, as an anti-acid.

MILLIBARS.
A unit of atmospheric pressure. A **BAR** is the air pressure which will support a column of mercury 75.007cm high. Normal atmospheric pressure is about 1.01325 bars or 1013.25 millibars.

MERCURY (Hg).
Mercury and its compounds are all poisonous. Mercury is a liquid, metallic element at room temperature. It is used in barometers, thermometers, mercury cells, mercury vapour lamps, and various laboratory equipment.

METAMORPHIC ROCK.
Rocks that have had their original physical nature changed by intense heat and/or pressure.

NICKEL (Ni).
Metallic element. Used in certain stainless steels and other special alloys, coinage and as a catalyst in the chemical industry.

NITRATES & NITRITES.
The salts of nitric acid (HNO_3) and nitrous acid (HNO_2) respectively. Some are important naturally occurring compounds such as saltpetre (potassium nitrate) and Chile saltpetre (sodium nitrate). Used in fertilisers and as a source of nitric acid.

OESOPHAGUS.
The muscular tube which carries swallowed food from the throat to the stomach. In adults it is approximately 30cm long.

ORE.
A mineral or combination of minerals from which metals or non-metals can be profitably extracted.

OZONE.
A very close relative of oxygen. It has the formula O_3 and can decompose readily to form normal oxygen O_2. It is this decomposition that also releases free oxygen atoms that makes ozone so dangerous to living organisms. It has a quite characteristic smell and might be noticed on the "dodgems" at a fairground where it is formed as a consequence of electrical discharge.

PANCREAS.
An elongated soft gland which lies slightly to the left behind the stomach. Its function is to provide enzymes which help in digestion and the hormone insulin which helps to control blood sugar levels.

PATHOGEN.
A micro-organism or substance that produces a disease.

PH-scale.
Is used to describe how acid something is. Acidic substances have a pH below 7, alkaline substances have a pH above 7 and neutral substances have a pH of 7.

PHOTOSYNTHESIS.
The chemical process that occurs in a green plant where carbon dioxide, water, sunlight and chlorophyll produce oxygen, glucose and starch.

POLYCHLORINATED BIPHENYLS (PCBs).
Compounds which were developed as insecticides. Based on combinations of benzene rings and chlorine atoms. Can be toxic to man. Difficult to separate so therefore their individual toxicities are not known. Have a long lifetime in the environment. Now very carefully controlled.

POTASSIUM SALTS.
Potassium is a very common metallic element found in the combined state. Most widely used are compounds such as potash (K_2CO_3) as a fertiliser, potassium chloride (KCl) used as a fertiliser, caustic potash (KOH) used to make detergents and soap, and potassium nitrate (KNO_3) used as a fertiliser and to make explosives and preservatives.

PRECIPITATION (CHEMICAL).
The formation of an insoluble solid by a chemical reaction which occurs in solution.

PRECIPITATION (ATMOSPHERIC).
Moisture falling onto the Earth's surface from clouds, i.e. rain, hail or snow.

PROTOZOA.
A phylum of unicellular organisms found extensively in marine and fresh water, free living or as parasites. Have the ability to move and some contain chlorophyll.

PROTEINS.
Organic compounds containing carbon, hydrogen, oxygen and nitrogen. They consist of hundreds of amino acid "building blocks". About twenty different amino acids can occur in proteins.

RENAL.
A medical term meaning related to the kidneys.

SALINE.
Salt or salty. Usually taken to mean the presence of the salts of sodium, potassium and magnesium. A typical example is salt itself, chemically known as sodium chloride (NaCl).

SEDIMENTARY ROCKS.
Rocks that have been formed by the compaction and cementing together of mineral and organic particles. These particles were formed by erosion at one or more places and deposited by wind, water, and glacial ice or precipitated from solution at another place.

SILICA.
A compound of silicon and oxygen of formula SiO_2. Sand is a form of silica. Silica forms about 94% of all rocks. It is used to make glass, ceramics and silicone materials.

SILICATES.
Materials which form a large part of the Earth's crust. Can have a very complex composition but all contain silicon, oxygen and one or more metals. Hydrogen may or may not be present.

SODIUM SALTS.
Sodium is a metallic element but is found normally in the combined state. Its occurrence is extensive. Salt is sodium chloride and is the starting point of many other materials. Caustic soda is sodium hydroxide which is used to make soap and detergents as well as plastics, dyes, etc.

TRACHEA.
Windpipe. It begins immediately below the voice-box (larynx) and runs down the centre of the front of the neck to end behind the upper part of the breast-bone (sternum). Here it divides to form the two main bronchi.

TRANSPIRATION.
The loss of water from the surfaces of leaves and other plant parts.

VOLATILE.
Changes readily to a vapour.

192

INDEX